Asian Words of Meaning

Reflections and thoughts on success, self-understanding and spiritual guidance from Asia's leading thinkers.

By

Steven Howard

Asian Words of Meaning

©2016 Steven Howard
All rights reserved.

No part of this Book may be reproduced or transmitted in any form or by any means, electronic or mechanical, including photocopying, recording, faxing, emailing, posting online or by any information storage and retrieval system, without written permission from the Author.

ISBN: 978-1-943702-06-0 (Print edition)
　　　　978-1-943702-07-7 (Kindle edition)

For reprint permission, please contact:
　　Steven Howard
　　c/o Caliente Press
　　1775 E Palm Canyon Drive, Suite 110-198
　　Palm Springs, CA   92264
　　U.S.A
　　Email: stevenhoward@verizon.net

Published by:
　　Caliente Press
　　1775 E Palm Canyon Drive, Suite 110-198
　　Palm Springs, CA 92264
　　U.S.A.
　　Email: CalientePress@verizon.net

Cover Design: Lee Chee Yih

Asian Words of Wisdom Series

The *Asian Words of Wisdom* series comprises the following titles:

Asian Words of Success — *Thoughts, quotations and phrases on leadership, marketing and personal development from Asia's leading thinkers.*

Asian Words of Meaning — *Reflections and thoughts on success, self-understanding and spiritual guidance from Asia's leading thinkers.*

Asian Words of Inspiration — *Thoughts, motivational quotes and wisdom from Asia's leading thinkers on personal and professional success and the journey of life.*

The Book of Asian Proverbs — *Unabridged collection of ancient sayings and teachings from across Asia.*

Indispensable Asian Words of Knowledge — *Words of wisdom from Asia's leading sages, philosophers, and statesmen.* (October 2016)

Asian Words of Meaning

Dedication

This book is dedicated to

Helen Lee

I have admired from afar

her spiritual foundations and roots,

which grant her keen insight into words of meaning.

Thank you for sharing your wisdom and knowledge

with all who know you.

Asian Words of Meaning

Asian Words of Meaning

Table of Contents

Introduction	9
Knowledge & Learning	13
Spiritual Guidance	37
Understanding Self	63
Life & Living	81
Success	113
Caring & Service to Others	147
About the Author	165

Asian Words of Meaning

Asian Words of Meaning

Introduction

Words and thoughts are often the great seeds that lead to personal change.

They are the building blocks that touch, provoke, arouse, and stir the individual passions and desires that stimulate personal motivation.

Within *Asian Words of Meaning* you will find nearly 800 motivational quotations, thoughts, and phrases from some of Asia's leading thinkers: Buddha, Confucius, Dalai Lama, Gandhi, Nisargadatta Maharaj, Lao-Tzu, Paramahansa Yogananda, Rumi and many others.

While we believe all of our sources for these quotations to be reliable, readers should not interpret *Asian Words of Meaning* as a highly researched, authoritative reference book. This is not what we set out to do and it is certainly not what we have delivered.

What we have set out to do is gather and share the quotes that moved us, impressed us, or got us thinking a bit harder, deeper, or even more lightly. In achieving this endeavor, we trust you will agree, *Asian Words of Meaning* does deliver.

While technically the continent of Asia extends all the way west to Turkey, most people today seem to cut Asia off at the western border of Pakistan. In truth, the boundaries of Asia are more culturally determined that geographic lines on maps and globes.

As such, I have elected to include a handful of quotes from Persia (modern Iran), as well as notable people and cultures from the Middle East and Arabian Gulf regions.

These quotations will provide the reader with a wealth of beliefs on spiritual guidance, understanding one's self, life, living, success, caring, service to others, and the pursuit of knowledge and learning.

Part of our *Asian Words of Wisdom* series, this book has been produced with a focal point on self-development and personal improvement. I hope you will take time to reflect upon the words and thoughts of these Asian leaders, and that the ideas found within *Asian Words of Meaning* will provide inspiration and motivation for your own personal growth and development.

Asian Words of Meaning

For, as Buddha wrote, *"Words have the power to both destroy and heal. When words are both true and kind they change our world."*

May these *Asian Words of Meaning* change your world and the world at large.

Steven Howard
August 2016

Asian Words of Meaning

Asian Words of Meaning

Knowledge & Learning

Knowledge, as defined by Plato, is *"justified true belief."*

His teacher Socrates, however, countered with *"knowledge is only perception."*

So, which is it? True belief or just a perception?

Asian sages have been writing about the importance of knowledge for centuries. And with the prevalence of the Internet in our daily lives, many people struggle with information overload and the problem of turning too much information into relevant knowledge and wisdom.

Western thinking about knowledge appears to focus on the functional, i.e. knowledge is only useful if it can be put to use to achieve something of importance or value.

In truth, knowledge should be appreciated for its own inherent attributes. Knowledge gained is a worthwhile acquisition in its own pursuit, whether or not it leads to some other attainment or result. After all, learning new knowledge should be driven primarily by internal motivations rather than external motivators.

Sharing of knowledge is human nature. In fact, the word *history* comes from a combination of the words *his* and *story*. Early man shared knowledge from generation to generation through a series of "his stories."

Our struggles today, as alluded to above, is that too much information is being shared, and not enough knowledge. Putting information into context that creates understanding and knowledge, and that leads to further learning, is very much needed in today's information overload world.

Of course today, many people understand the importance of *lifelong learning* and understand that what is learned in the formal classroom during one's formative years is often not sufficient (nor necessarily important) in later life. This is one reason why people realize late in life (sometimes too late) that life experiences are as valuable as educational resources.

Continuous learning is crucial to continuous personal growth. All of life, from birth to death, is a continuous process of learning. How we each turn these lessons of life into personal knowledge, however, differs greatly. Some make the requisite connections, others fail to find these indispensable links.

Asian Words of Meaning

The linkage between knowledge and learning may have been best summarized by Confucius, who wrote, *"To be fond of learning is to be near knowledge."*

Perhaps the knowledge and wisdom found in the quotes below will provide insight, meaning, knowledge, and vital connection points for your life's experiences and journey.

Know then that true knowledge does not create a new being for you; it only removes your "ignorant ignorance."
Sri Ramana Maharshi

You must understand the whole of life, not just one little part of it. That is why you must read, that is why you must look at the skies, that is why you must sing and dance, and write poems and suffer and understand, for all that is life.
Jiddu Krishnamurti

Everything has its beauty but not everyone sees it.
Confucius

Only the wisest and stupidest of men never change.
Confucius

Asian Words of Meaning

Learn as if you will live forever. Live as if you will die tomorrow.
> Mohandas Karamchand (Mahatma) Gandhi

He who learns but does not think, is lost! He who thinks but does not learn is in great danger!
> Confucius

When the student is ready, the master appears.
> Buddhist Proverb

Wisdom is not negation of anything.
> Swami Krishnananda Saraswati

The knowledge which purifies the mind and the heart alone is true knowledge, all else is only a negation of knowledge.
> Sri Ramakrishna

This I conceive to be the chemical function of humor: to change the character of our thought.
> Lin Yutang

When you lose, don't lose the lesson.
> Dalai Lama

Asian Words of Meaning

Learning is like rowing upstream: not to advance is to drop back.
Chinese Proverb

Better than a thousand days of diligent study is one day with a great teacher.
Japanese Proverb

By three methods we may learn wisdom: first, by reflection, which is noblest; second, by imitation, which is easiest; and third by experience, which is the bitterest.
Confucius

When you can do nothing, what can you do?
Zen Kōan

As the bee takes the essence of a flower and flies away without destroying its beauty and perfume, so let the sage wander in this life.
The Dhammapada

Man becomes that of which he thinks.
The Upanishads

The man who's drunk water knows if it's cool or warm.
Zen Proverb

Asian Words of Meaning

Through a difficult period you can learn, you can develop inner strength, determination and courage to face the problems.

Dalai Lama

Anger and intolerance are the twin enemies of correct understanding.

Mohandas Karamchand (Mahatma) Gandhi

The intellect delights in investigating the past and the future but does not look to the present. Environment, time, and objects are all in oneself. How can they exist independently of me? They may change, but "I" remain unchanging.

Sri Ramana Maharshi

The purely agitational attitude is not good enough for a detailed consideration of a subject.

Jawaharlal Nehru

Facts are facts and will not disappear on account of your likes.

Jawaharlal Nehru

Gravity is only the bark of wisdom; but it preserves it.

Confucius

Asian Words of Meaning

Logic and cold reason are poor weapons to fight fear and distrust. Only faith and generosity can overcome them.

Jawaharlal Nehru

He who merely knows right principles is not equal to him who loves them.

Confucius

The quieter you become the more you can hear.

Baba Ram Dass

Knowledge is merely brilliance in organization of ideas and not wisdom. The truly wise person goes beyond knowledge.

Confucius

The bird of wisdom needs two wings to fly. They are awareness and equanimity.

Satya Narayan Goenka

Believe nothing, no matter where you read it, or who said it, even if I have said it, unless it agrees with your own reason and your own common sense.

Buddha

Asian Words of Meaning

Those who have knowledge, don't predict. Those who predict, don't have knowledge.

Lao-Tzu

Chi Wen Tzu always thought three times before taking action. Twice would have been quite enough.

Confucius

Words must be used like stepping stones: lightly and with nimbleness, because if you step on them too heavily, you incur the danger of falling into the intellectual mire of logic and reason.

Ramesh S. Balsekar

We want our dreams to come true but is the value in dreams or truth?

Swami Amar Jyoti

It is not necessary to meet your guru on the physical plane. The guru is not external.

Neem Karoli Baba

Pass beyond form, escape from names! Flee titles and names toward meaning!

Rumi

Asian Words of Meaning

A scholar who cherishes the love of comfort is not fit to be deemed a scholar.

Lao-Tzu

Freedom from the desire for an answer is essential to the understanding of a problem.

Jiddu Krishnamurti

It is precisely for the reason that Truth is utterly simple, basic, elementary, and totally obvious, that it is completely overlooked.

Ramesh S. Balsekar

Look for the answer inside your question.

Rumi

Ignorance is the night of the mind, but a night without moon or star.

Confucius

The essence of knowledge is, having it, to apply it; not having it, to confess your ignorance.

Confucius

Tao is labor lost.

Confucius

Asian Words of Meaning

Acquire new knowledge whilst thinking over the old, and you may become a teacher of others.

Confucius

A theory must be tempered with reality.

Jawaharlal Nehru

When you have spoken the word, it reigns over you. When it is unspoken you reign over it.

Arabian Proverb

It is man that makes truth great, not truth that makes man great.

Confucius

Realize that no matter how wonderful a situation may be, its nature is such that it must end.

Dalai Lama

As is the food, so is the Mind,
As is the mind, so are the Thoughts,
As are the thoughts, so is the Conduct,
As is the conduct, so is the Health.

Sai Baba

Asian Words of Meaning

Knowing ignorance is strength; ignoring knowledge is sickness.

Lao-Tzu

A powerful interest which dominates a man's life polarizes his mind, which then acts like a magnet and continually draws out from his stored-up experience and also from new experiences whatever is relevant and useful to the end in view. Deep interest invigorates the mind, awakens its dormant powers and is the key to super excellence, invention and discovery.

Swami Krishnananda Saraswati

All living beings are connected and ultimately inseparable, and we should learn to listen and communicate with each other.

Dalai Lama

Disillusionment arises due to a discrepancy between the way a situation appears to be and the way it actually is.

Dalai Lama

Once you get the value of your own tradition, then you can see the value of other traditions more easily.

Dalai Lama

Asian Words of Meaning

Use intelligence positively, live holistically, and open yourselves to a more positive experience. Automatically our minds become more widened.

Dalai Lama

At 15 I set my heart upon learning.
At 30, I planted my feet firm upon the ground.
At 40, I no longer suffered from perplexities.
At 50, I knew what were the biddings of Heaven.
At 60, I heard them with docile ear.
At 70, I could follow the dictates of my own heart; for what I desired no longer overstepped the boundaries of right.

Confucius

Study without thinking and you are blind; think without studying and you are in danger.

Confucius

Two monks were describing a flapping flag. One said: "The flag is moving." The other said: "The wind is moving." Hui Neng happened to be passing by. He said "Not the wind, not the flag; the mind is moving."

Zen Kōan

Asian Words of Meaning

The mind of man is the root of both bondage and release.

                                            Paramahansa Yogananda

Three things cannot be long hidden — the sun, the moon, and the truth.

                                                         Confucius

I have noticed that nothing I have never said ever did me any harm.

                    Mohandas Karamchand (Mahatma) Gandhi

Solitude is in the mind of man. One might be in the thick of the world and maintain serenity of mind. Such a one is in solitude. Another may stay in a forest but still be unable to control his mind. Such a man cannot be said to be in solitude. Solitude is a function of the mind. A man attached to desires cannot get solitude wherever he may be, whereas a detached man is always in solitude.

                                        Sri Ramana Maharshi

It is not so much what you believe in that matters, it is more the way in which you believe it and proceed to translate that belief into action.

                                                        Lin Yutang

Asian Words of Meaning

Words have the power to both destroy and heal. When words are both true and kind they can change our world.

Buddha

The more man meditates upon good thoughts, the better will be his world and the world at large.

Confucius

Teachers open the door, but you must enter by yourself.

Chinese Proverb

Silence is a great help to a seeker after truth.

Mohandas Karamchand (Mahatma) Gandhi

Imagining is like feeling around in a dark lane. You are the truth from foot to brow. Now, what else would you like to know?

Rumi

To know that you do not know is the best. To pretend to know when you do not know is a disease. Only when one recognizes this disease as a disease can one be free from the disease.

Lao-Tzu

Asian Words of Meaning

A man must elevate himself by his own mind, not degrade himself. The mind is the friend of the conditioned soul, and his [potential] enemy as well.

Bhagavad Gita

Large skepticism leads to large understanding. Small skepticism leads to small understanding. No skepticism leads to no understanding.

Wang Xi Zhi

They must often change, who would be constant in happiness or wisdom.

Confucius

Let a hundred flowers bloom, let a hundred schools of thought contend.

Mao Zedong

Evil exists to glorify the good. Evil is negative good. It is a relative term. Evil can be transmuted into good. What is evil to one at one time, becomes good at another time to somebody else.

Mencius

Asian Words of Meaning

Freedom from the desire for an answer is essential to the understanding of a problem.

Jiddu Krishnamurti

In oneself lies the whole world and if you know how to look and learn, the door is there and the key is in your hand. Nobody on earth can give you either the key or the door to open, except yourself.

Jiddu Krishnamurti

So when you are listening to somebody, completely, attentively, then you are listening not only to the words, but also to the feeling of what is being conveyed, to the whole of it, not part of it.

Jiddu Krishnamurti

There is no need to education. It is not that you read a book, pass an examination, and finish with education. The whole of life, from the moment you are born to the moment you die, is a process of learning.

Jiddu Krishnamurti

Real knowledge is to know the extent of one's ignorance.

Confucius

Asian Words of Meaning

What is needed, rather than running away or controlling or suppressing or any other resistance, is understanding fear; that means, watch it, learn about it, come directly into contact with it. We are to learn about fear, not how to escape from it.

Jiddu Krishnamurti

When we talk about understanding, surely it takes place only when the mind listens completely — the mind being your heart, your nerves, your ears — when you give your whole attention to it.

Jiddu Krishnamurti

It is only the wisest and the very stupidest who cannot change.

Confucius

There are three truths: my truth, your truth, and the truth.

Chinese Proverb

The sages do not consider that making no mistakes is a blessing. They believe, rather, that the great virtue of man lies in his ability to correct his mistakes and continually make a new man of himself.

Wang Yang-Ming

Asian Words of Meaning

Refresh your connection, but not with talking. You have secretly refreshed your desires. As long as desires are fresh, connection is not; for it is these desires that lock that gate.

Rumi

The golden rule of conduct is mutual toleration, seeing that we will never all think alike and we shall always see truth in fragment and from different points of vision.

Mohandas Karamchand (Mahatma) Gandhi

Rewards and punishments are the lowest form of education.

Chuang Tzu

Be vigilant. Guard your mind against negative thoughts.

Buddha

Do not dwell on the past, do not dream of the future, concentrate the mind on the present moment.

Buddha

A single conversation across the table with a wise man is worth a month's study of books.

Chinese Proverb

Asian Words of Meaning

You are the witness of thought as it rises and passes away and stops. The one who watches is everlasting.
Hariwansh Lal (Papaji) Poonja

We all cling to the past, and because we cling to the past we become unavailable to the present.
Osho

If you can be independent of the world, then you can see oneness in everything. The difference of opposites is the obstacle that prevents you from seeing oneness in everything because the opposites do not exist in oneness; they cease to be opposites in oneness. Oneness is positive in its entirety.
Swami Krishnananda Saraswati

Everything has beauty, but not everyone sees it.
Confucius

When the shoe fits, the foot is forgotten; when the belt fits, the belly is forgotten; when the heart is right, "for" and "against" are forgotten.
Chuang Tzu

Ignorance is the night of the mind, but a night without moon or star.
Confucius

Asian Words of Meaning

The expectations of life depend upon diligence; the mechanic that would perfect his work must first sharpen his tools.

> Confucius

Knowledge manifested, wisdom grows. Wisdom manifested, spirituality soars.

> Sri Chinmoy

True thoughts have duration in themselves.
If the thoughts endure, the seed is enduring;
If the seed endures, the energy endures;
If the energy endures, then will the spirit endure.
The spirit is thought; thought is the heart; the heart is the fire; the fire is the Elixir.

> Lu Yen

If you are a minority of one, the truth is the truth.

> Mohandas Karamchand (Mahatma) Gandhi

Silence is the true friend that never betrays.

> Confucius

Enlightenment must come little by little — otherwise it would overwhelm.

> Indries Shah

Asian Words of Meaning

Meditation brings wisdom; lack of meditation leaves ignorance. Know well what leads you forward and what holds you back, and choose the path that leads to wisdom.

Buddha

Kites harness the force of the wind.
They express our intent,
But they cannot change the wind.

Zen Proverb

Discard every self-seeking motive as soon as it is seen and you need not search for truth. Truth will find you.

Nisargadatta Maharaj

Those who have knowledge of the natural way do not train themselves in cunning, whilst those who use cunning to rule their lives, and the lives of others, are not knowledgeable of the Tao, nor of natural happiness.

Lao-Tzu

Truth at all costs.
Mohandas Karamchand (Mahatma) Gandhi

Everything happens together by itself.
Ramesh S. Balsekar

Asian Words of Meaning

Our own life is the instrument with which we experiment with truth.

Thich Nhat Hanh

Learning is weightless, a treasure you can always carry easily.

Chinese Proverb

When you are deluded and full of doubt, even a thousand books of scripture are not enough. When you have realized understanding, even one word is too much.

Fen-Yang

They who know the truth are not equal to those who love it. They who love it are not equal to those who delight in it.

Confucius

Great knowledge sees all in one. Small knowledge breaks down into the many.

Chuang Tzu

The superior man understands what is right; the inferior man understands what will sell.

Confucius

The ink of the scholar is more holy than the blood of the martyr.

Prophet Muhammad

Asian Words of Meaning

When the mind discriminates, there is manifoldness of things; when it does not, it looks into the true state of things.
Buddhist Proverb

It is not so much what you believe in that matters, as the way in which you believe it and proceed to translate that belief into action.
Lin Yutang

Anything truly revolutionary is created by a few who see what is true and are willing to live according to that truth; but to discover what is true demands freedom from tradition, which means freedom from all fears.
Krishnamurti

Tell me, I forget. Show me, I remember. Involve me, I understand.
Confucius

Silence is the true *upadesa* (teaching). It is the perfect *upadesa*. It is suited only for the most advanced seeker. The others are unable to draw full inspiration from it. Therefore they require words to explain the truth. But truth is beyond words. It does not admit of explanation. All that is possible to do is to indicate it.
Sri Ramana Maharshi

Asian Words of Meaning

To perceive things in the germ is intelligence.

Lao-Tzu

When you know a thing, hold that you know it. When you know not a thing, allow that you know it not. This is knowledge.

Confucius

Asian Words of Meaning

Spiritual Guidance

Many of the world's greatest religions and philosophies have their roots and foundations in Asia, each seeking to give meaning and purpose to life and the lives of its followers.

These religions and philosophies include:

> Buddhism — established in northern India about 2500 years ago in response to the life and teachings of Siddhārtha Gautama, who was given the title Buddha or awakened one. This philosophy of life has spread throughout the world and has subdivided into numerous distinct groups.

> Confucian — a great tradition with a highly developed emphasis on ethics, ritual, and learning. This philosophy derives from the life and teachings of Master Kung and has had a very great influence on Chinese culture, both within China and the Chinese diaspora.

Asian Words of Meaning

Hinduism — the dominant religion of the Indian subcontinent and the third largest religion in the world after Christianity and Islam. Established over 3000 years ago, Hinduism is based on ancient scriptures known collectively as the *Vedas*. Hindus believe in a supreme spiritual force called Brahman with which an individual will become one after cleansing his or her karma through a cycle of birth, death, and rebirth. In life Hindus follow the laws of *dharma*, or spiritual teachings.

I Ching — a form of divination and transformation first revealed in the *Book of Changes* around 700 BC. The *I Ching* is the most ancient form of practical advice and metaphysical wisdom and has been the basis for many philosophies and belief systems over the years. To this day the *I Ching* provides guidance to those seeking true organization and balance of the Universe's natural elements. The *yin* and *yang*, representing all the possible sets of naturally paired opposites, is incorporated into this philosophical work, which has become part history and part eternal spiritual guide.

Jainism — presents nature in the purest and truest form. Jainism is as old as nature, which has neither a beginning nor an end. The mission of Jainism is the mission of nature, which is to work for the welfare of one and all, to rise from the pitfall of ignorance and inaction, to the spiritual climax of infinite bliss and perfect knowledge.

Shinto — the traditional *Way of the Gods* in Japan. Shinto does not have a founder nor does it have sacred scriptures like the *sutras* or the bible. Deeply rooted in the Japanese people and tradition, *Shinto Gods* are called **kami**. They are sacred spirits which take the form of things and concepts important to life, such as wind, rain, mountains, trees, rivers, and fertility. Humans become *kami* after they die and are revered by their families as ancestral *kami*. In contrast to many monotheist religions, there are not absolutes in Shinto. There is no absolute right and wrong, and nobody is perfect. Shinto is an optimistic faith, as humans are thought to be fundamentally good, and evil is believed to be caused by evil spirits. Consequently, the purpose of most Shinto rituals is to keep away evil spirits by purification, prayers, and offerings to the *kami*.

Sikhism — a progressive religion well ahead of its time when it was founded over 500 years ago. The Sikh religion today has a following of roughly 30 million people worldwide and is ranked as the world's 5th largest religion. Sikhism preaches a message of devotion and remembrance of the all-pervading spirit (god) at all times, truthful living, equality of mankind, and denounces superstitions and blind rituals.

Taoism — an ancient Chinese religion and philosophy that sees the universe as engaged in ceaseless motion and activity. All is considered to be in continual flux. The universe is intrinsically dynamic. This continual cosmic process is called the *Tao* by the Chinese. The process is described in terms of *Yin* and *Yang*. Taoism celebrates humanity as a part of the circulation of the energies of nature. Traditional medical techniques and martial arts (such as *Tai Chi*) are consistent with Taoist traditions. Later Taoism became highly institutionalized and ritualized, with priestly specialists who conduct funerals and other basic rites for their religious clients.

Zen — is a school of Mahayana Buddhism that originated in China during the Tang Dynasty, spread across North and Southeast Asia, and is now practiced globally. Strongly influenced by Taoism, Zen emphasizes rigorous meditation practice. Its focus is insight into the Buddha-nature and how the personal expression of this insight into daily life can benefit the practitioner and others.

Asian Words of Meaning

I am convinced that reading the wise words below will help you cement your own personal religious and spiritual beliefs, no matter what these are.

May these words enlighten you and help you along on your own personal spiritual journey.

Just as a candle cannot burn without fire, men cannot live without a spiritual life.

Buddha

God has no religion.

Mohandas Karamchand (Mahatma) Gandhi

There is no need for temples, no need for complicated philosophy. Our own brain, our own heart is our temple; the philosophy is kindness.

Dalai Lama

The secret of health for both mind and body is not to mourn for the past, not to worry about the future, or not to anticipate troubles, but to live the present moment wisely and earnestly.

Buddha

Asian Words of Meaning

Prayer carries us halfway to God, fasting brings us to the door of His palace, and alms-giving procures us admission.
The Koran

Seeking blessings from outsiders is not right. Your life is on your own shoulders. Blind faith is not healthy.
Dalai Lama

Freedom from conditioning comes with the freedom from thinking. When the mind is utterly still, only then is there freedom for the real to be.
Thich Nhat Hanh

God comes to the hungry in the form of food.
Mohandas Karamchand (Mahatma) Gandhi

In matters of conscience, the law of majority has no place.
Mohandas Karamchand (Mahatma) Gandhi

At any moment, you have a choice, that either leads you closer to your spirit or further away from it.
Thich Nhat Hanh

When I let go of what I am, I become what I might be.
Lao-Tzu

Asian Words of Meaning

A realized one sends out waves of spiritual influence in his aura, which draw many people towards him. Yet he may sit in a cave and maintain complete silence.

                                              Sri Ramana Maharshi

The joke is that it is the ego, the "me" that wants enlightenment, and enlightenment cannot come until the "me" is demolished.

                                              Ramesh S. Balsekar

The pure heart is the best mirror for the reflection of truth. All truth in the universe will manifest in your heart, if you are sufficiently pure.

                                              Swami Vivekananda

Devotion without understanding is only emotion and later becomes a passion: fanaticism.

                                      Swami Krishnananda Saraswati

It is vital to realize that understanding is all, that there is no question of altering, or amending what is, and that therefore the question of any method or technique for "attaining" enlightenment is totally irrelevant.

                                              Ramesh S. Balsekar

Asian Words of Meaning

Zen is not a particular state but the normal state: silent, peaceful, unagitated. In *Zazen* neither intention, analysis, specific effort, nor imagination take place. It's enough just to be without hypocrisy, dogmatism, arrogance — embracing all opposites.

Taisen Deshimaru

Your degree of absence of thought is your measuring stick on the spiritual path.

Ramana Maharshi

The body is your temple. Keep it pure and clean for the soul to reside in.

B.K.S. Iyengar

Faith is an oasis in the heart which will never be reached by the caravan of thinking.

Kahlil Gibran

The lover of this world is like someone in love with a wall illuminated by sunrays; he doesn't realize that the radiance and the splendor do not come from the wall but from the sun. He gives his heart to the wall and when at sunset the rays of sun disappear, he is in despair.

Rumi

Asian Words of Meaning

When you purify your hearts just as you purify your raiment, union with God will follow. You cannot become a Sufi by merely wearing coarse woolen shirts and following strict ritual, pretending to be pious while inside your hearts you bear malice and avarice. A real Sufi has attained a state of perfection on the inside. If you sincerely seek union with God, then seek Him inside your hearts and leave the world alone.

Sheikh Abdul-Qadir Jilani

God is not hiding! When you do not see God it is only because you are looking elsewhere. So you must absolutely see God and nothing else. Then it is God that is looking through your eyes.

Hariwansh Lal (Papaji) Poonja

Our life is a long and arduous quest after Truth and the soul requires inward restfulness to attain its full height.

Mohandas Karamchand (Mahatma) Gandhi

The various religions are like different roads converging on the same point. What difference does it make if we follow different routes, provided we arrive at the same destination?

Mohandas Karamchand (Mahatma) Gandhi

Asian Words of Meaning

Spiritual advancement is not to be measured by one's display of outward powers, but solely by the depth of his bliss in meditation.

Paramahansa Yogananda

The more awake one is to the material world, the more one is asleep to spirit. When our soul is asleep to God, other wakefulness closes the door of Divine grace.

Rumi

Words that enlighten the soul are more precious than jewels.

Inayat Khan

Dive deep; one does not get to the precious gems by merely floating on the surface. God is without form, no doubt; but He also has a form. By meditating on God with form one speedily acquires devotion; then one can meditate on the formless God. It is like throwing a letter away after learning its contents, then setting out to follow its instructions.

Ramakrishna Paramahamsa

The soul which cannot endure fire and smoke won't find the Secret.

Rumi

Asian Words of Meaning

Oh you who have gone astray, why are you searching all over the world? He is not outside you. Why search for Him?

Rumi

There are degrees of the ascent of consciousness. You don't jump into something at once. Gradually, you move from the lesser, or the more external, to the higher, and the more internal. From the external, you move to the internal; from the internal, you move to the Universal. These are the three stages of spiritual ascent.

Swami Krishnananda Saraswati

Forge your spirit through actual practice and experience. Your spirit is not your slave. It needs nourishment.

Awa Kenzo
Zen Bow, Zen Arrow

O Spirit, teach me to pray and pray, with deep concentration. O Spirit, balance my meditation with devotion, and purify my devotion with all-surrendering love unto Thee.

Swami Yogananda

Silence is the true friend that never betrays.

Confucius

Asian Words of Meaning

We feel that we can exercise our volition, yet deep down we know that there is an order infinitely more powerful which seems to dictate our life.

Ramesh S. Balsekar

The soul that moves in the world of the senses and yet keeps the senses in harmony, free from attraction and aversion, finds rest in quietness.

Bhagavad Gita

The mind that turns ever outward will have no end to craving. Only the mind turned inward will find a still-point of peace.

Tao Te Ching

To the mind that is still, the whole universe surrenders.

Lao-Tzu

Born to be wild — live to outgrow it.

Lao-Tzu

Silence is a source of great strength.

Lao-Tzu

Great acts are made up of small deeds.

Lao-Tzu

From caring comes courage.

Lao-Tzu

Asian Words of Meaning

The end of pain lies not in pleasure. When you realize that you are beyond both pain and pleasure, are aloof and unassailable, then the pursuit of happiness ceases and the resultant sorrow too. For pain aims at pleasure and pleasure ends in pain, relentlessly.

Nisargadatta Maharaj

The undisturbed state of being is bliss; the disturbed state is what appears as the world. In non-duality there is bliss; in duality there is experience. What comes and goes is experience, with its duality of pain and pleasure. Bliss is not to be known. One is always in bliss, but never blissful. Bliss is not an attribute.

Nisargadatta Maharaj

As many faiths, so many paths.

Sri Ramakrishna

When the Spirit is known, and when we know of ourselves as the Spirit; there is no land or sea, no earth or sky — all is He.

Paramahansa Yogananda

When meditation is mastered, the mind is unwavering like the flame of a lamp in a windless place.

Bhagavad Gita

Asian Words of Meaning

It is felt that a disciplined mind leads to happiness and an undisciplined mind leads to suffering, and in fact it is said that bringing about discipline within one's mind is the essence of the Buddha's teaching.

Dalai Lama

Training of the mind helps one to bear sorrows and bereavements with courage, and finally these do not affect such one.

Sri Ramana Maharshi

What one looks for outside turns out to be present inside, but only to be discovered after a long detour of seeking externally, in all the wrong places….in a process of gradual reversal, the return of what moves forward in the shape of a circle, in which the end meets the initial point of departure.

Zhang Longxi

It's best not to get too excited or too depressed by the ups and downs of life.

Dalai Lama

Since you harbor ill will, it has a negative impact on yourself. You may lose your appetite and good sleep.

Dalai Lama

Asian Words of Meaning

Every pleasure, physical or mental, needs an instrument. Both the physical and mental instruments are materials, they get tired and worn out. The pleasure they yield is necessarily limited in intensity and duration. Pain is the background of all your pleasures. You want them because you suffer. On the other hand, the very search for pleasure is the cause of pain. It is a vicious circle.

Nisargadatta Maharaj

My experience is that everything is bliss. But the desire for bliss creates pain. Thus bliss becomes the seed of pain. The entire universe of pain is born of desire. Give up the desire for pleasure and you will not even know what is pain.

Nisargadatta Maharaj

It is difficult for me to regard anyone who obeys no moral principle in his conduct to be a religious man.

Mohandas Karamchand (Mahatma) Gandhi

All religions carry same teaching, same goal, same potential.

Dalai Lama

When we have an inner peace, we can be at peace with those around us.

Dalai Lama

Asian Words of Meaning

If you don't find God in the next person you meet, it is a waste of time looking for him further.

                       Mohandas Karamchand (Mahatma) Gandhi

God is seated in the hearts of all.

                       Bhagavad Gita

Meditation brings wisdom; lack of meditation leaves ignorance. Know well what leads you forward and what holds you back, and choose the path that leads to wisdom.

                       Buddha

You cannot buy peace of mind in a shop — at least not as long as our brains haven't been replaced by computers.

                       Dalai Lama

When one is in the highest transcendental *samadhi*, the physical personality of others disappears. We do not see others as human beings. We see only a flow of consciousness, like a river that is entering into the ocean.

                       Sri Chinmoy

One who knows the truth sees everyone else as a manifestation of God.

                       Sri Ramana Maharshi

Asian Words of Meaning

Yoga is the control of thought waves in the mind.

Patañjali

Do not dwell in the past, do not dream of the future, concentrate the mind on the present moment.

Buddha

Spirituality is like a medicine. To heal the illness, it is not sufficient to look at the medicine and talk about it. You have to ingest it.

Dalai Lama

Prayer is the key of the morning and the bolt of the evening.

Mohandas Karamchand (Mahatma) Gandhi

He who is contented is rich.

Lao-Tzu

Prayer is a confession of one's own unworthiness and weakness.

Mohandas Karamchand (Mahatma) Gandhi

The willing contemplation of vice is vice.

Arabian Proverb

Asian Words of Meaning

To see and listen to the wicked is already the beginning of wickedness.

Confucius

There is nothing that wastes the body like worry, and one who has any faith in God should be ashamed to worry about anything whatsoever.

Mohandas Karamchand (Mahatma) Gandhi

Nirvana is not the blowing out of the candle. It is the extinguishing of the flame because day is come.

Rabindranath Tagore

Every child comes with the message that God is not yet discouraged of man.

Rabindranath Tagore

Call on God, but row away from the rocks.

Indian Proverb

The whole secret of existence is to have no fear. Never fear what will become of you, depend on no one. Only the moment you reject all help are you freed.

Buddha

Asian Words of Meaning

The soul loves to meditate, for in contact with the Spirit lies its greatest joy. If, when you experience mental resistance during meditation, remember that reluctance to meditate comes from the ego; it doesn't belong to the soul.

Paramahansa Yogananda

Darkness reigns at the foot of the lighthouse.

Japanese Proverb

As the fletcher whittles and makes straight his arrows, so the master directs his straying thoughts.

Buddha

He who talks more is sooner exhausted.

Lao-Tzu

Muddy water, let stand — becomes clear.

Lao-Tzu

Great souls have wills; feeble souls have only wishes.

Chinese Proverb

All that we are is the result of what we have thought. If a man speaks or acts with an evil thought, pain follows him. If a man speaks or acts with a pure thought, happiness follows him, like a shadow that never leaves him.

Buddha

Asian Words of Meaning

Consciousness is the basis of all life and the field of all possibilities. Its nature is to expand and unfold its full potential. The impulse to evolve is thus inherent in the very nature of life.

Maharishi Mahesh Yogi

To me God is truth and love, God is ethics and morality, God is fearlessness.

Mohandas Karamchand (Mahatma) Gandhi

Inner tranquility comes from the development of love and compassion.

Dalai Lama

Renunciation is always in the mind, not in going to forests or solitary places, or giving up one's duties. The main thing is to see that the mind does not turn outward but inward. It does not really rest with a man whether he goes to this place or that or whether he gives up his duties or not. All these events happen according to destiny. All the activities that the body is to go through are determined when it first comes into existence. It does not rest with you to accept or reject them. The only freedom you have is to turn your mind inward and renounce activities there.

Sri Ramana Maharshi

Asian Words of Meaning

Human beings are of such nature that they should have not only material facilities but spiritual sustenance as well. Without spiritual sustenance, it is difficult to get and maintain peace of mind.

Dalai Lama

The path may not be left for an instant. If it could be left, it would not be the path.

Confucius

The farther you go, the less you know.

Lao-Tzu

Remember that not getting what you want is sometimes a wonderful stroke of luck.

Dalai Lama

When one makes the mind stick to one thought, the mind becomes rock-steady and the energy is conserved.

Sri Ramana Maharshi

Meditation is sticking to one thought. That single thought keeps away other thoughts; distraction of mind is a sign of its weakness; by constant meditation it gains strength.

Sri Ramana Maharshi

Asian Words of Meaning

The allness created pain and sorrow that happiness might show itself by contrast for hidden things are made manifest by means of their opposites: since the allness has no opposite, it is hidden.

Rumi

Those who are free of resentful thoughts surely find peace.

Buddha

You are awareness. Awareness is another name for you. Since you are Awareness there is no need to attain or cultivate it. All that you have to do is to give up being aware of other things, that is of not-self. If one gives up being aware of them then pure awareness alone remains, and that is the Self.

Sri Ramana Maharshi

He who wherever he goes is attached to no person and to no place by ties of flesh; who accepts good and evil alike, neither welcoming the one nor shrinking from the other — take it that such a one has attained Perfection.

Bhagavad Gita

Life finds its purpose and fulfilment in the expansion of happiness.

Maharishi Mahesh Yogi

Asian Words of Meaning

Patient and regular practice is the whole secret of spiritual realization. Do not be in a hurry in spiritual life. Do your utmost, and leave the rest to God.

> Swami Sivananda Saraswati

The mind creates misery for itself even when there is pleasure. Both pleasure and pain are therefore mental creations.

> Sri Ramana Maharshi

For us the highest purpose of this world is not merely living in it, knowing it and making use of it, but realizing our own selves in it through expansion of sympathy; not alienating ourselves from it and dominating it, but comprehending and uniting it with ourselves in perfect union.

> Rabindranath Tagore

It is good to be born in a church, but it is bad to die there. It is good to be born a child, but bad to remain a child. Churches, ceremonies, symbols are good for children; but when the child is grown up, he must burst, either the church or himself. The end of all religion is the realization of God.

> Swami Vivekananda

Asian Words of Meaning

When we speak of being highly developed spiritually, this does not mean we float in the air. In fact, the higher we go, the more we come down to earth.

Chogyam Trungpa

In the attitude of silence the soul finds the path in a clearer light, and what is elusive and deceptive resolves itself into crystal clearness.

Mohandas Karamchand (Mahatma) Gandhi

People become speechless at the sight of the trees, the flowers, the pond. But, alas how few are they who seek the owner of all these?

Ramakrishna Paramahamsa

All existence is a manifestation of God…..We imagine that the soul is in the body, almost a result and derivation from the body; but it is the body that is in the soul and a result and derivation from the soul.

Sri Aurobindo

Asian Words of Meaning

Asian Words of Meaning

Understanding Self

According to Buddhist legend, it was under the peepal tree (*Ficus religiosa*, a species of fig) in Bodhgaya that Siddhārtha Gautama, who became the Buddha, took his last seat as an ordinary self-centered person and attained unexcelled perfect enlightenment.

While few of us can realistically expect to attain the enlightenment achieved by Buddha, a desire and striving for better self-understanding exists within all of us.

There is a wide range of means that can facilitate the self-enlightenment experience. Though the means may vary, the intent behind the means is quite narrowly defined as the intent to expand into a state of integration whereby all aspects of your conscious self become increasingly aligned with your divine essence.

This divine essence is defined as the fullest expression of the soul, and most closely exemplifies the self's capabilities therein.

Asian Words of Meaning

Some writers believe that there are three particular life principles that help to align your perspective with the perspective of divine essence and thus inspire the self-enlightenment experience.

These are seeing the Divine in all, nurturance of life, and gratitude.

When you apply these principles, a deeper meaning will be revealed to the seemingly random events of your life experience. This concept is incorporated, in various fashion, in most Asian religious and philosophical thought.

For instance, in the practice of Zen as a way of life, a slow, deliberate development through mental and moral purification is encompassed in thought, word, and deed. This process, created centuries ago, has at its core the continued learning about one's self through rigorous meditation practices and inner reflection.

Likewise, much of Indian philosophical thought has been focused on the desire and need for self-awareness and self-understanding.

Perhaps the words in this chapter will be a guide and an inspiration for your own attainment of self-understanding and self-definition.

Asian Words of Meaning

Be conscious of yourself, watch your mind, give it your full attention. Don't look for quick results; there may be none within your noticing.

Nisargadatta Maharaj

Self-Realization is effortless. What you are trying to find is what you already are.

Ramesh Balsekar

Men cannot see their reflection in running water, but only in still water.

Chuang Tzu

To know the mind is the most important task of your life. And to know the mind is to know the world.

Buddhist Proverb

It is the human mind that creates its own difficulties and then cries for help.

Sri Ramana Maharshi

Bliss is not added to your nature; it is merely revealed as your true and natural state, eternal and imperishable.

Sri Ramana Maharshi

Asian Words of Meaning

The only way to be rid of your grief is to know and be the self.

Sri Ramana Maharshi

Meditation is not sitting and fidgeting, daydreaming, worrying, or fantasizing. It means watching, calmly observing the mind itself. Calm observation makes the mind itself calmer.

Swami Rama

If you think that you are bound, you remain bound; you make your own bondage. If you know that you are free, you are free this moment. This is knowledge, knowledge of freedom. Freedom is the goal of all nature.

Swami Vivekananda

Self-realization and the knowledge of God are synonymous.

Swami Kriyananda

The source of all creation is pure consciousness….pure potentiality seeking expression from the unmanifest to the manifest. And when we realize that our true Self is one of pure potentiality, we align with the power that manifests everything in the universe.

Deepak Chopra

Asian Words of Meaning

Forgetting your self is the greatest injury; all the calamities flow from it. Take care of the most important, the lesser will take care of itself. You do not tidy up a dark room. You open the windows first. Letting in the light makes everything easy. So, let us wait with improving others until we have seen ourselves as we are — and have changed. There is no need to turn round and round in endless questioning; find yourself and everything will fall into its proper place.

Nisargadatta Maharaj

The self cannot be found in books. You have to find it for yourself, within yourself.

Sri Ramana Maharshi

My objective is not to get rid of the ego, simply to be aware of how it leads me and where.

Deepak Chopra

If you had a choice you would never let go of the illusion.

Ram Tzu

I am learning to be patient and compassionate with myself as I gain the courage to be true to myself.

Shakti Gawain

Asian Words of Meaning

What you are, you already are. By knowing what you are not, you are free of it and remain in your own natural state. It all happens quite spontaneously and effortlessly.

Nisargadatta Maharaj

As long as you derive inner help and comfort from anything, keep it.

Mohandas Karamchand (Mahatma) Gandhi

The highest form of human intelligence is to observe yourself without judgment.

Krishnamurti

Self-enquiry is the direct path to Self-realization or enlightenment. The only way to make the mind cease its outward activities is to turn it inward. By steady and continuous investigation into the nature of the mind, the mind itself gets transformed into That to which it owes its own existence.

Ramesh S. Balsekar

You are misled if you think the self is easy to subdue.

Rumi

Asian Words of Meaning

One who knows much about others may be learned, but one who understands himself is more intelligent. One who controls others may be powerful, but one who has mastered himself is mightier still.

Lao-Tzu

Don't look for help from someone other than yourself. The remedy for your wound is the wound itself.

Rumi

When you become stabilized in your Self, the continuous commentary of the mind will stop. Your true state is ever-existent.

Nisargadatta Maharaj

When you are inspired by some great purpose, some extraordinary project, all your thoughts break their bounds. Dormant forces, faculties and talents become alive, and you discover yourself to be a greater person by far than you ever dreamed yourself to be.

Patañjali

The mystic dances in the sun, hearing music others don't. "Insanity," they say. If so, it's a very gentle, nourishing sort.

Rumi

Asian Words of Meaning

Remember: if you can cease all restless activity, your integral nature will appear.

Hua Hu Ching

We are what we think. All that we are arises with our thoughts. With our thoughts we make the world. Speak or act with a pure mind and happiness will follow you as your shadow, unshakeable.

The Dhammapada

The only devils in this world are those running around in our own hearts, and that is where all our battles should be fought.

Mohandas Karamchand (Mahatma) Gandhi

The ultimate state of mind is clear light, but its clarity can be covered up by negative emotional states such as anger, hatred, or anxiety.

Dalai Lama

Work is no hindrance to realization. It is the mistaken identity of the doer with non-self that troubles him. Get rid of the false identity.

Sri Ramana Maharshi

Asian Words of Meaning

Knowing others is wisdom, knowing yourself is enlightenment.

Lao-Tzu

All that we are is the result of what we have thought. The mind is everything. What we think, we become.

Buddha

It's sheer illusion to try to separate the phenomena from the reality, and then try to love phenomena first. It just doesn't happen that way, so naturally we end in failure. You don't have to try to achieve unity with others. It is fallacious thinking and doing. Realize the unity of everything and everyone within you first.

Swami Amar Jyoti

The outward freedom that we shall attain will only be in exact proportion to the inward freedom to which we may have grown at a given moment. And if this is a correct view of freedom, our chief energy must be concentrated on achieving reform from within.

Mohandas Karamchand (Mahatma) Gandhi

Asian Words of Meaning

I have lived on the lip of insanity, wanting to know reasons, knocking on a door. It opens. I've been knocking from the inside!

Rumi

The mind is like a monkey swinging from branch to branch through the forest. In order not to lose sight of the monkey, we must watch the monkey constantly and even be one with it.

Thich Nhat Hanh

If you have controlled your mind you are the conqueror of the whole world.

Swami Sivananda Saraswati

Curb your tongue and senses, and you are beyond trouble. Let them loose and you are beyond help.

Lao-Tzu

Purity of mind and idleness are incompatible.

Mohandas Karamchand (Mahatma) Gandhi

Not to have control over the senses is like sailing in a rudderless ship, bound to break to pieces on coming into contact with the very first rock.

Mohandas Karamchand (Mahatma) Gandhi

Asian Words of Meaning

We shape clay into a pot, but it is the emptiness inside that holds whatever we want.

Tao Te Ching

The secret to inner peace is nothing more mysterious than healthy mental attitudes.

Dalai Lama

It is a man's own mind, not his enemy or foe, that lures him to evil ways.

Buddha

Realize yourself as the ocean of consciousness in which all happens. This is not difficult. A little attentiveness or close observation of yourself and you will see that no event is outside your consciousness.

Nisargadatta Maharaj

Forget the known, but remember that you are the knower. Don't be all the time immersed in your experiences. Remember that you are beyond the experiencer, ever unborn and deathless. In remembering it, the quality of pure knowledge will emerge, the light of unconditional awareness.

Nisargadatta Maharaj

Asian Words of Meaning

You should examine yourself daily. If you find faults, you should correct them. When you find none, you should try even harder.

Wang Xi Zhi

Every duty is a charge, but the charge of oneself is the root of all others.

Mencius

Blaming your faults on your nature does not change the nature of your faults.

Indian Proverb

Mind is merely a collection of thoughts, or a collection of impressions which makes up this "me", this self image.

Ramesh Balsekar

True happiness cannot be found in things that change and pass away. Pleasure and pain alternate inexorably. Happiness comes from the self and can be found in the self only. Find your real self and all else will come with it.

Nisargadatta Maharaj

The snow goose need not bathe to make itself white. Neither need you do anything but be yourself.

Lao-Tzu

Asian Words of Meaning

To be aware is to be awake. Unaware means asleep. You are aware anyhow, you need not try to be. What you need is to be aware of being aware. Be aware deliberately and consciously, broaden and deepen the field of awareness. You are always conscious of the mind, but you are not aware of yourself as being conscious.

Nisargadatta Maharaj

The more we become independent of our mind, compelling it to silence, the better servant it becomes, and the more useful the services it can render to us in its own sphere of action.

Mouni Sadhu

It is our own mental attitude, which makes the world what it is for us. Our thoughts make things beautiful, our thoughts make things ugly. The whole world is in our own minds. Learn to see things in the proper light.

Swami Vivekananda

The way is not in the sky.
The way is in the heart.

Buddha

Asian Words of Meaning

Anger will never disappear so long as thoughts of resentment are cherished in the mind. Anger will disappear just as soon as thoughts of resentment are forgotten.

Buddha

Health is the greatest gift, contentment the greatest wealth, faithfulness the best relationship.

Buddha

Your own Self-Realization is the greatest service you can render the world.

Sri Ramana Maharshi

This is the ultimate end of man, to find the One which is in him; which is his truth, which is his soul; the key with which he opens the gate of the spiritual life, the heavenly kingdom.

Rabindranath Tagore

Let a man strive to purify his thoughts. What a man thinketh, that is he; this is the eternal mystery. Dwelling within himself with thoughts serene, he will obtain imperishable happiness. Man becomes that of which he thinks.

The Upanishads

Asian Words of Meaning

We are formed and molded by our thoughts. Those whose minds are shaped by selfless thoughts give joy when they speak or act. Joy follows them like a shadow that never leaves them.

Buddha

Peace comes from within. Do not seek it without.

Buddha

It is your mind that has separated the world outside your skin from the world inside and put them in opposition. This created fear and hatred and all the miseries of living.

Nisargadatta Maharaj

There is no chaos in the world except the chaos which your mind creates.

Nisargadatta Maharaj

Harmony between the inner and the outer is happiness. On the other hand, self-identification with the outer causes suffering.

Nisargadatta Maharaj

Many could forgo heavy meals, a full wardrobe, a fine house, et cetera; it is the ego they cannot forgo.

Mohandas Karamchand (Mahatma) Gandhi

Asian Words of Meaning

Desires are just waves in the mind. You know a wave when you see one. A desire is just a thing among many. I feel no urge to satisfy it, no action needs to be taken on it. Freedom from desire means this: the compulsion to satisfy is absent.

Nisargadatta Maharaj

Paradise is surrounded by what we dislike; the fires of hell by what we desire.

Rumi

People who seek the way observe their own mind. When you know Buddha is within, and do not seek it outside yourself, then mind itself is Buddha and Buddha is the mind.

Fu Shanhui

The mind is empty infinity, infinite emptiness, full of possibilities.

Mumon Yamada Roshi

It is unwise to be too sure of one's own wisdom. It is healthy to be reminded that the strongest might weaken and the wisest might err.

Mohandas Karamchand (Mahatma) Gandhi

Asian Words of Meaning

What the superior man seeks is in himself; what the small man seeks is in others.

Confucius

A quiet mind is all you need. All else will happen rightly, once your mind is quiet. As the sun on rising makes the world active, so does self-awareness affect changes in the mind. In the light of calm and steady self-awareness, inner energies wake up and work miracles without any effort on your part.

Nisargadatta Maharaj

You are fighting with yourself. You have to resolve it, not fight with it. Resolve, dissolve, solve.

Swami Amar Jyoti

Training of the mind helps one to bear sorrows and bereavements with courage and finally these do not affect such a wise one.

Sri Ramana Maharshi

Emotional reactions, born of ignorance or inadvertence, are never justified. Seek a clear mind and a clean heart. Keep quietly alert, enquiring into the real nature of yourself. This is the only way to peace.

Nisargadatta Maharaj

Asian Words of Meaning

The idea of enlightenment is of utmost importance. Just to know that there is such a possibility changes one's entire outlook. It acts like a burning match in a heap of sawdust. All the great teachers did nothing else.

Nisargadatta Maharaj

Nearly all mankind is more or less unhappy because nearly all do not know the true Self. Real happiness abides in Self-knowledge alone. All else is fleeting. To know one's Self is to be blissful always.

Sri Ramana Maharshi

One may gain political and social independence, but if one is a slave to his passions and desires, one cannot feel the pure joy of real freedom.

Swami Vivekananda

No one can see their reflection in running water. It is only in still water that we can see.

Taoist Proverb

Asian Words of Meaning

Life & Living

All cultures and societies create rules and guidelines for how people should live their lives. But even in collectivist societies, individuals still seek their own paths and set their own directions.

Confucius was once asked, "Is there one word which may serve as a rule of practice for all one's life?" He replied: "Is not reciprocity such a word? What you do not want done to yourself, do not do to others."

Asian cultures with belief systems such as Confucianism, Taoism, and Buddhism stress harmonious relations with the world. They see no real separation between people and their natural environment, and their beliefs allow them to live at peace with it.

Perhaps the most familiar Asian way of creating balance in life is the philosophy of *Feng Shui*. Practiced for over 3000 years, the purpose of *Feng Shui* (literally "wind and water") is to bring balance, harmony, and beneficial energy to the environment where we live and work. Today, this art and science is used by millions of people worldwide and continues to grow in popularity as people experience its benefits.

In ancient China, the *Feng Shui* master was a spiritual master as well. He studied the forces of nature, the direction and force of the wind and water, the surrounding elements, the qualities of *yin* and *yang*, the seasons, the earth energies, the quality of the land, the building materials, and the direction of the building in order to maximize the vital energy, or *Ch'i*, of the dwelling. Each factor was crucial in building an auspicious place to live, worship, or work.

In *Feng Shui* there are three basic principles that define *Ch'i*, the energy that animates, connects, and moves everything through the cycles of life:

- All things in the physical world are endowed with living energy known as *Ch'i*.

- *Ch'i* connects every physical thing.

- The *Ch'i* in everything is constantly changing.

Asian Words of Meaning

The goal of *Feng Shui* is to create living environments that are comfortable, organized, and in harmony with our inner being.

We hope the words and thoughts below will lead to greater balance in your own life and living environment, as well as a greater focus on reciprocity.

Life is really simple, but we insist on making it complicated.
>   Confucius

People deal too much with the negative, with what is wrong. Why not try and see positive things, to just touch those things and make them bloom?
>   Thich Nhat Hanh

If you are planning for one year, grow rice. If you are planning for 20 years, grow trees. If you are planning for centuries, grow men.
>   Chinese Proverb

We cannot all do great things, but we can do small things with great love.
>   Mother Teresa

Asian Words of Meaning

The future depends on what we do in the present.
> Mohandas Karamchand (Mahatma) Gandhi

If you are patient in one moment of anger, you will escape a hundred days of sorrow.
> Chinese Proverb

What is the worth of a happiness for which you must strive and work? Real happiness is spontaneous and effortless.
> Nisargadatta Maharaj

Just as every action that emanates from us comes back to us as reaction, even so our actions may act on other people and theirs on us.
> Swami Vivekananda

We have all been created for the sole purpose to love and be loved.
> Mother Teresa

To understand everything is to forgive everything.
> Buddha

One filled with joy preaches without preaching.
> Mother Teresa

Asian Words of Meaning

When you are content to be simply yourself and don't compare or compete, everyone will respect you.
Lao-Tzu

Permanent good can never be the outcome of untruth and violence.
Mohandas Karamchand (Mahatma) Gandhi

The most powerful thing you can do to change the world is to change your own beliefs about the nature of life, people, reality, to something more positive.
Shakti Gawain

Love and compassion are necessities, not luxuries. Without them humanity cannot survive.
Dalai Lama

If you cry because the sun has gone out of your life, your tears will prevent you from seeing the stars.
Rabindranath Tagore

No matter how much you nurse a grudge, it won't get better.
Lao-Tzu

Asian Words of Meaning

You will not be punished for your anger, you will be punished by your anger.

                                                  Buddha

When you are in the right, you can afford to keep your temper; when you are in the wrong, you can't afford to lose it.

                    Mohandas Karamchand (Mahatma) Gandhi

Anger and intolerance are the enemies of correct understanding.

                    Mohandas Karamchand (Mahatma) Gandhi

We have so committed ourselves in different ways that we have hardly any time for self-reflection, to observe, to study.

                                    Jiddu Krishnamurti

Hatred does not cease by hatred, but only by love; this is the eternal rule.

                                                  Buddha

Many people think excitement is happiness. But when you are excited you are not peaceful. True happiness is based on peace.

                                          Thich Nhat Hanh

Asian Words of Meaning

To be idle is a short road to death and to be diligent is a way of life; foolish people are idle, wise people are diligent.

Buddha

In the dojo, aim for truth.
At home, aim for harmony.
At work, aim for progress.
Among friends, aim for trust.
In the world, aim for sincerity.

Awa Kenzo
Zen Bow, Zen Arrow

We can solve many problems in an appropriate way, without any difficulty, if we cultivate harmony, friendship, and respect for one another.

Dalai Lama

Happiness is your nature. It is not wrong to desire it. What is wrong is seeking it outside when it is inside.

Sri Ramana Maharshi

When small men begin to cast big shadows, it means that the sun is about to set.

Lin Yutang

Asian Words of Meaning

Try again, no matter how many times you have failed. Always try once more.

> Paramahansa Yogananda

Three things cannot be long hidden: the sun, the moon, and the truth.

> Buddha

One joy scatters a hundred griefs.

> Chinese Proverb

Life is suffering. Once you learn to accept that life is suffering, life will cease to be suffering.

> Buddha

We often suffer because we do not understand. Understanding is a great thing; once we understand, we can tolerate.

> Inayat Khan

They must often change, who would be constant in happiness or wisdom.

> Confucius

Asian Words of Meaning

Sometimes your joy is the source of your smile, but sometimes your smile can be the source of your joy.

Thich Nhat Hanh

Laughter is the language of the Gods.

Buddhist Proverb

Laws control the lesser man. Right conduct controls the greater one.

Chinese Proverb

If you do not change direction, you may end up where you are heading.

Lao-Tzu

When starting out on a great journey, it is important to start from where you are now and not from where you think you should be.

Yogi Satyananda Saraswati

We are here to awaken from the illusion of our separateness.

Thich Nhat Hanh

It is vital that when educating our children's brains that we do not neglect to educate their hearts.

Dalai Lama

Asian Words of Meaning

Such is human psychology that if we don't express our joy, we soon cease to feel it.

Lin Yutang

Happiness is when what you think, what you say, and what you do are in harmony.

Mohandas Karamchand (Mahatma) Gandhi

There is more to life than increasing its speed.

Mohandas Karamchand (Mahatma) Gandhi

New beginnings are often disguised as painful endings.

Lao-Tzu

If you correct your mind, the rest of your life will fall into place.

Lao-Tzu

What the caterpillar calls the end, the rest of the world calls a butterfly.

Lao-Tzu

What you are seeking is seeking you.

Rumi

Asian Words of Meaning

Those who are free of resentful thoughts surely find peace.
— Buddha

No matter how hard the past, you can always begin again.
— Buddha

Those who flow as life flows know they need no other force.
— Lao-Tzu

When you think everything is someone else's fault, you will suffer a lot. When you realize that everything springs only from yourself, you will learn both peace and joy.
— Dalai Lama

Care about what other people think and you will always be their prisoner.
— Lao-Tzu

Children learn to smile from their parents.
— Shinichi Suzuki

Smile at each other, smile at your wife, smile at your husband, smile at your children, smile at each other — it doesn't matter who it is — and that will help you to grow up in greater love for each other.
— Mother Teresa

Asian Words of Meaning

A family is a place where minds come in contact with one another. If these minds love one another the home will be as beautiful as a flower garden. But if these minds get out of harmony with one another it is like a storm that plays havoc with the garden.

Buddha

To enjoy good health, to bring true happiness to one's family, to bring peace to all, one must first discipline and control one's own mind. If a man can control his mind he can find the way to Enlightenment, and all wisdom and virtue will naturally come to him.

Buddha

In dwelling, live close to the ground. In thinking, keep to the simple. In conflict, be fair and generous. In governing, don't try to control. In work, do what you enjoy. In family life, be completely present.

Lao-Tzu

If you correct your mind, the rest of your life will fall into place.

Lao-Tzu

Asian Words of Meaning

Do not sit long with a sad friend. When you go to a garden, do you look at thorns or flowers? Spend more time with roses and jasmine.

Rumi

What you are is what you have been. What you will be is what you do now.

Buddha

Life can be really and truly simple if we don't fight it.

Ramesh S. Balsekar

If you look to others for fulfillment, you will never truly be fulfilled.

Lao-Tzu

Do not let the behavior of others destroy your inner peace.

Dalai Lama

Holding on to anger is like grasping a hot coal with the intent of throwing it at someone else; you are the one who gets burned.

Buddha

Asian Words of Meaning

To educate people for peace, we can use words or we can speak with our lives.

                                          Thich Nhat Hanh

No one ever won a chess game by betting on each move. Sometimes you have to move backward to get a step forward.

                                          Amar Gopal Bose

We can never obtain peace in the outer world until we make peace with ourselves.

                                          Dalai Lama

When you make a choice, you change the future.

                                          Deepak Chopra

There is no key to happiness. The door is always open.

                                          Mother Teresa

If you conduct your life on the basis of truth and honesty, it gives you a sense of satisfaction and self-confidence.

                                          Dalai Lama

There is no best path or worst path. There is just the path to which each individual gets directed.

                                          Ramesh S. Balsekar

Asian Words of Meaning

There is no path to happiness; happiness is the path.

Buddha

Besides the noble art of getting things done, there is the noble art of leaving things undone. The wisdom of life consists in the elimination of non-essentials.

Lin Yutang

The trouble is, you think you have time.

Buddha

See the positive side, the potential. And make an effort.

Dalai Lama

What the world wants is character.

Swami Vivekananda

Those who don't feel this life pulling them like a river, those who don't drink dawn like a cup of spring water or take in the sunset like supper, those who don't want to change, let them sleep.

Rumi

Be gentle with the earth.

Dalai Lama

Asian Words of Meaning

Man and his deed are two distinct things. Whereas a good deed should call forth approbation, and a wicked deed disapprobation, the doer of the deed, whether good or wicked always deserves respect or pity as the case may be.

                Mohandas Karamchand (Mahatma) Gandhi

Freedom is not worth having if it does not include the freedom to make mistakes.

                Mohandas Karamchand (Mahatma) Gandhi

The world will right itself; take the long view and you are comforted.

                Lin Yutang

Approach love and cooking with reckless abandon.

                Dalai Lama

The secret of contentment is the discovery by every man of his own powers and limitations, finding satisfaction in a line of activity which he can do well, plus the wisdom to know that his place, no matter how important or successful he is, never counts very much in the universe.

                Lin Yutang

Asian Words of Meaning

I have learned through bitter experience the one supreme lesson to conserve my anger, and as heat conserved is transmitted into energy, even so our anger controlled can be transmitted into a power that can move the world.

                Mohandas Karamchand (Mahatma) Gandhi

Morality is the attunement of oneself to the atmosphere one finds oneself in at any time. It is always changing with the evolutionary process to which the individual is subject. Morality is relative from place to place, time to time, but the necessity for morality is absolute.

                Swami Krishnananda Saraswati

When the mind is at peace, the world too is at peace. You are neither holy nor wise, just an ordinary fellow who has completed his work.

                Layman Pang

To live a pure unselfish life, one must count nothing as one's own in the midst of abundance.

                Buddha

Some people like to make of life a garden, and to walk only within its paths.

                Japanese Proverb

Asian Words of Meaning

Choosing between kindness and unkindness, you should try to act always with a kind heart and forsake cold-heartedness.

                                        Dalai Lama

It is the nature of human beings to yearn for freedom, equality, and dignity. If we accept that others have a right to peace and happiness equal to our own, do we not have a responsibility to help those in need?

                                        Dalai Lama

Let us leave the lotus blossom as it is. It blooms when it blooms, it falls when it falls. Now it stands up in full blossom under the clear blue sky, and the entire cosmos is reflected in it. Neither the Buddha nor Kasyapa can touch that — nor can we. It simply greets us in the soft breeze and awaits our quiet and respectful smile.

                                  Takeuchi Yoshinori

If you must play, decide on three things at the start: the rules of the game, the stakes and the quitting time.

                                  Chinese Proverb

What is man's ultimate direction in life? It is to look for love, truth, virtue, and beauty.

                                  Shinichi Suzuki

Asian Words of Meaning

I think the human hand is meant for embracing and not for hitting.

Dalai Lama

Every human being has the potential to create either a happy or a miserable life.

Dalai Lama

The vast accumulation of material wealth during the twentieth century has not led to human happiness.

Dalai Lama

What you do is of little significance; but it is very important that you do it.

Mohandas Karamchand (Mahatma) Gandhi

We live in a wonderful world that is full of beauty, charm, and adventure. There is no end to the adventures that we can have if only we seek them with our eyes open.

Jawaharlal Nehru

The woman who tells her age is either too young to have anything to lose or too old to have anything to gain.

Chinese Proverb

Asian Words of Meaning

It is the habit of every aggressor nation to claim that it is acting on the defensive.
Jawaharlal Nehru

The art of a people is a true mirror of their minds.
Jawaharlal Nehru

No culture can live, if it attempts to be exclusive.
Mohandas Karamchand (Mahatma) Gandhi

Culture is the widening of the mind and the spirit.
Jawaharlal Nehru

Culture of the mind must be subservient to the heart.
Mohandas Karamchand (Mahatma) Gandhi

There is no fire like passion, there is no shark like hatred, there is no snare like folly, there is no torrent like greed.
Buddha

Hatred does not cease by hatred, but only by love; this is the eternal rule.
Buddha

Asian Words of Meaning

A hundred men may make an encampment, but it takes a woman to make a home.
Chinese Proverb

A coward is incapable of exhibiting love; it is the prerogative of the brave.
Mohandas Karamchand (Mahatma) Gandhi

The history of the world is full of men who rose to leadership, by sheer force of self-confidence, bravery, and tenacity.
Mohandas Karamchand (Mahatma) Gandhi

I always pray that the good core of our human character — which cherishes truth, peace, and freedom — will prevail.
Dalai Lama

Peace will not come from the sky.
Dalai Lama

Soaring economic growth could not replace spiritual satisfaction, which is the key to life.
Dalai Lama

Govern a family as you would cook a small fish — very gently.
Chinese Proverb

Asian Words of Meaning

Life is not a continuum of pleasant choices, but of inevitable problems that call for strength, determination, and hard work.

Indian Proverb

Only mad dogs and Englishmen go out in the noonday sun.

Indian Proverb

You must not lose faith in humanity. Humanity is an ocean. If a few drops of the ocean are dirty, the ocean does not become dirty.

Mohandas Karamchand (Mahatma) Gandhi

We part at the crossroads,
You leave with your joys and problems,
I, with mine. Alone, I look down the road.
Each one must follow one's own path.

Tao Te Ching

Nature can provide for the needs of people; [she] can't provide for the greed of people.

Mohandas Karamchand (Mahatma) Gandhi

Mankind fears an evil man but heaven does not.

Mencius

Asian Words of Meaning

Old age, believe me, is a good and pleasant thing. It is true you are gently shouldered off the stage, but then you are given such a comfortable front stall as spectator.

Confucius

Where there are too many policemen, there is no liberty. Where there are too many soldiers, there is no peace. Where there are too many lawyers, there is no justice.

Lin Yutang

Whenever you take a step forward, you are bound to disturb something. You disturb the air as you go forward, you disturb the dust, the ground. You trample upon things. When a whole society moves forward, this trampling is on a much bigger scale; and each thing that you disturb, each vested interest which you want to remove, stands as an obstacle.

Indira Gandhi

Yesterday is a dream, tomorrow but a vision. But today well lived makes every yesterday a dream of happiness and every tomorrow a vision of hope. Look well therefore to this day.

Sanskrit Proverb

When you have faults, do not fear to abandon them.

Confucius

Asian Words of Meaning

Peace is not a relationship of nations. It is a condition of mind brought about by a serenity of soul. Lasting peace can come only to peaceful people.

Jawaharlal Nehru

The wisdom of life consists in the elimination of nonessentials.

Lin Yutang

To divide and particularize is in the mind's very nature. There is no harm in dividing. But separation goes against fact. Things and people are different, but they are not separate. Nature is one, reality is one. There are opposites, but no opposition.

Nisargadatta Maharaj

Praise and blame
gain and loss
pleasure and sorrow
come and go like the wind.
To be happy,
rest like a great tree in the midst of them all.

Buddha

Asian Words of Meaning

Life is an opportunity, benefit from it.
Life is a beauty, admire it.
Life is a dream, realize it.
Life is a challenge, meet it.
Life is a duty, complete it.
Life is a game, play it.
Life is a promise, fulfill it.
Life is sorrow, overcome it.
Life is a song, sing it.
Life is a struggle, accept it.
Life is a tragedy, confront it.
Life is an adventure, dare it.
Life is luck, make it.
Life is life, fight for it!

Mother Teresa

If early death is common in the land, and if death is meted out as punishment, the people do not fear to break the law. To be the executioner in such a land as this, is to be as an unskilled carpenter who cuts his hand when trying to cut wood.

Lao-Tzu

Violence never settles anything.

Genghis Khan

Asian Words of Meaning

Man learns through experience, and the spiritual path is full of different kinds of experiences. He will encounter many difficulties and obstacles, and they are the very experiences he needs to encourage and complete the cleansing process.

Sai Baba

If there is light in the soul, there will be beauty in the person. If there is beauty in the person, there will be harmony in the house. If there is harmony in the house, there will be order in the nation. If there is order in the nation, there will be peace in the world.

Chinese Proverb

Age considers; youth ventures.

Rabindranath Tagore

A humanity at peace will know the endless fruits of victory, sweeter to the taste than any nurtured on the soil of blood.

Paramahansa Yogananda

Monotony is the law of nature. Look at the monotonous manner in which the sun rises. The monotony of necessary occupations is exhilarating and life-giving.

Mohandas Karamchand (Mahatma) Gandhi

Asian Words of Meaning

The satiated man and the hungry one do not see the same thing when they look upon a loaf of bread.
Rumi

It is easy enough to be friendly to one's friends. But to befriend the one who regards himself as your enemy is the quintessence of true religion. The other is mere business.
Mohandas Karamchand (Mahatma) Gandhi

The effects of our actions may be postponed but they are never lost. There is an inevitable reward for good deeds and an inescapable punishment for bad. Reflect upon this truth, and seek always to earn good wages from Destiny.
Wu Ming Fu

When I'm trusting and being myself as fully as possible, everything in my life reflects this by falling into place easily, often miraculously.
Shakti Gawain

A great man is he who has not lost the heart of a child.
Mencius

Asian Words of Meaning

The main purpose of life is to live rightly, think rightly, act rightly. The soul must languish when we give all our thought to the body.

                        Mohandas Karamchand (Mahatma) Gandhi

Fool me once, shame on you. Fool me twice, shame on me.

                        Chinese Proverb

The best politics is right action.

                        Mohandas Karamchand (Mahatma) Gandhi

Nothing in the world is meaningless. Everything has a reason or a meaning to it. Therefore, be happy and smile. Everything is divinity charged with the Divine Absolute.

                        Swami Krishnananda Saraswati

Meditate silently. You will be able to create a totally new life for yourself.

                        Sri Chinmoy

Thinkers do not accept the inevitable; they turn their efforts toward changing it.

                        Paramahansa Yogananda

Asian Words of Meaning

He is poor who does not feel content.

Japanese Proverb

There are two great forces in the universe, silence and speech. Silence prepares, speech creates. Silence acts, speech gives the impulse to action. Silence compels, speech persuades.

Sri Aurobindo

Once upon a time a man whose axe was missing suspected his neighbor's son. The boy walked like a thief, looked like a thief, and spoke like a thief. But the man found his axe while digging in the valley, and the next time he saw his neighbor's son, the boy walked, looked, and spoke like any other child.

Lao-Tzu

It is only when we silent the blaring sounds of our daily existence that we can finally hear the whispers of truth that life reveals to us, as it stands knocking on the doorsteps of our hearts.

K.T. Jong

It is the nature of reason to see the end; it is the nature of desire not to.

Rumi

Asian Words of Meaning

Let us rise up and be thankful, for if we didn't learn a lot today, at least we learned a little, and if we didn't learn a little, at least we didn't get sick, and if we got sick, at least we didn't die; so, let us all be thankful.

Buddha

Fiery lust is not diminished by indulging it, but inevitably by leaving it ungratified. As long as you are laying logs on the fire, the fire will burn. When you withhold the wood, the fire dies.

Rumi

The more man meditates upon good thoughts, the better will be his world and the world at large.

Confucius

Words have the power to both destroy and heal. When words are both true and kind, they can change our world.

Buddha

Civilization, in the real sense of the term, consists not in the multiplication but in the deliberate and voluntary reduction of wants.

Mohandas Karamchand (Mahatma) Gandhi

Asian Words of Meaning

If we are to teach real peace in this world, and if we are to carry on a real war against war, we shall have to begin with the children.
                Mohandas Karamchand (Mahatma) Gandhi

Unity, to be real, must stand the severest strain without breaking.
                Mohandas Karamchand (Mahatma) Gandhi

Permanent good can never be the outcome of untruth and violence.
                Mohandas Karamchand (Mahatma) Gandhi

Happiness comes when your work and words are of benefit to yourself and others.
                Buddha

The secret of health for both mind and body is not to mourn for the past, worry about the future, or anticipate troubles but to live in the present moment wisely and earnestly.
                Buddha

No culture can live if it attempts to be exclusive.
                Mohandas Karamchand (Mahatma) Gandhi

Asian Words of Meaning

Men earn money. Men spend money. Money spends the man.

Thakur Dass Bhatia

The mind is the cause of bondage and liberation for all mankind.

Maitri Upanishad

Love is the only reality and it is not a mere sentiment. It is the ultimate truth that lies at the heart of creation.

Rabindranath Tagore

Life's fulfilment finds constant obstacles in its path; but those are necessary for the sake of its advance. The stream is saved from the sluggishness of its current by the perpetual opposition of the soil through which it must cut its way. The spirit of fight belongs to the genius of life.

Rabindranath Tagore

Life's journey is the reward.

Chinese Proverb

Anticipate the difficult by managing the easy.

Lao-Tzu

Asian Words of Meaning

Success

A Google search on the word *success* results in almost 1.2 billion web page results.

There are entire industries built around teaching, motivating, explaining, rewarding, awarding, describing, and depicting success.

Everyone has his or her own definition of success. And, it seems, almost everyone has something to say about success — a Google search on the phrase "success quotes" produces over 176 million Internet links.

With success being a favorite topic for all mankind, it should not be surprising to find that this has been a much loved and favorite subject matter for many Asian sages, thinkers, and philosophers.

I hope the quotations and phrases in this section on success will help you to achieve your own personal and professional levels of success.

Asian Words of Meaning

To be able under all circumstances to practice five things constitutes perfect virtue; these five things are gravity, generosity of soul, sincerity, earnestness, and kindness.

Confucius

Opportunities multiply as they are seized.

Sun Tzu

To see what is right and not to do it is cowardice.

Confucius

There is nothing noble in being superior to some other man. The true nobility is in being superior to your previous self.

Hindu Proverb

He who would go a hundred miles should consider ninety-nine as halfway.

Japanese Proverb

The weak can never forgive. Forgiveness is the attribute of the strong.

Mohandas Karamchand (Mahatma) Gandhi

The future depends on what we do in the present.

Mohandas Karamchand (Mahatma) Gandhi

Asian Words of Meaning

Honesty is the gateway to success; it is indeed 50% of success. Learning is not necessary, no need to be learned. All that you have to do is to be sure and sincere that you are crying for Oneness only and nothing else. Let the aim of life be clear in your mind, first. I repeat, your aim should be nothing other than the Ultimate Reality.

                      Swami Krishnananda Saraswati

If you want to do real work, give your whole heart to it. Nothing happens just by talking. A drop of water inside the house is better than a gushing river outside.

                      Rumi

In order to pursue your goals with your whole heart, you must have a vision. In turn, your vision must be fueled by a deep seated belief that you will succeed. This means that sometimes you have to look beyond all the facts and go with your gut instinct. Unfortunately, other people will often view this act of courage, this act of faith in yourself, as unrealistic. I strongly disagree. As long as you believe in yourself and in your success, anything is possible. Don't wait for others to give you the go-ahead on your dreams. Trust yourself to succeed and you will.

                      Sri Ramana Maharshi
                      Absolute Consciousness

Asian Words of Meaning

The superior man makes the difficulty to be overcome his first interest; success comes only later.

> Confucius

Put your heart, mind, intellect, and soul even to your smallest acts. This is the secret of success.

> Swami Sivananda Saraswati

Success often comes to those who dare to act. It seldom goes to the timid who are ever afraid of the consequences.

> Jawaharlal Nehru

Judge your success by what you had to give up in order to get it.

> Dalai Lama

Every great mistake has a halfway moment, a split second when it can be recalled and perhaps remedied.

> Pearl S. Buck

Nature's intelligence functions with effortless ease....with carefreeness, harmony, and love. And when we harness the forces of harmony, joy, and love we create success and good fortune with effortless ease.

> Deepak Chopra

Asian Words of Meaning

Fame or integrity: which is more important?

Money or happiness: which is more valuable?

Success or failure: which is more destructive?

If you look to others for fulfillment, you will never truly be fulfilled.

If your happiness depends on money, you will never be happy with yourself.

Be content with what you have; rejoice in the way things are.

When you realize that nothing is lacking, the whole world belongs to you!

Lao-Tzu

Doubt is a thought that interferes with the manifestation of desire. I do not let it be the director of my life.

Deepak Chopra

Success should be measured by the yardstick of happiness; by your ability to remain in peaceful harmony with cosmic laws.

Paramahansa Yogananda

Asian Words of Meaning

When his good deeds overcome his bad, a man gives light to the world like the moon breaking free from behind the clouds.

The Dhammapada

Winners compare their achievements with their goals, while losers compare their achievements with those of other people.

Nido Qubein

If you do not change direction, you may end up where you are heading.

Lao-Tzu

Before embarking on important undertakings sit quietly, calm your senses and thoughts and meditate deeply. You will then by guided by the creative power of Spirit. After that you should utilize all necessary means to achieve your goal.

Paramahansa Yogananda

Use only that which works and take it from any place you can find it.

Bruce Lee

Asian Words of Meaning

Your work is to discover your world and then with all your heart give yourself to it.
Buddha

Men's natures are alike; it is their habits that separate them.
Confucius

Man's attitude is the secret of life, for it is upon man's attitude that success and failure depend. Both man's rise and fall depend upon his attitude.
Inayat Khan

Action to be effective must be directed to clearly conceived ends.
Jawaharlal Nehru

It is not he who has spoken a hundred words aloud who has won; it is he who has perhaps spoken only one word.
Inayat Khan

Happiness comes when your work and words are of benefit to yourself and others.
Buddha

Fashion your life as a garland of beautiful deeds.
Buddha

Asian Words of Meaning

You cannot change the course of events, but you can change your attitude and what really matters is the attitude and not the bare event.

Nisargadatta Maharaj

Be not afraid of growing slowly; be afraid only of standing still.

Chinese Proverb

We live in the present, we dream of the future, but we learn eternal truths from the past.

Madame Chiang Kai-shek

We must embrace pain and burn it as fuel for our journey.

Miyazawa Kenji

Whenever you are confronted with an opponent conquer him with love.

Mohandas Karamchand (Mahatma) Gandhi

To live in obscurity, and yet practice wonders, in order to be mentioned with honor in future ages — this is what I do not do.

Confucius

Asian Words of Meaning

The softest things in the world overcome the hardest things in the world.

                                                  Lao-Tzu

The difference between what we do, and what we are capable of doing, would solve most of the world's problems.

                      Mohandas Karamchand (Mahatma) Gandhi

He who possesses sincerity is he who, without an effort, hits what is right and apprehends without the exercise of thought; he is the sage who naturally and easily embodies the right way. He who attains to sincerity is he who chooses what is good, and firmly holds it fast.

                                               Confucius

I have always believed that the company name is the life of an enterprise. It carries responsibility and guarantees the quality of the product.

                                            Akio Morita

The superior man thinks always of virtue; the common man thinks of comfort.

                                               Confucius

You can't shake hands with a clenched fist.

                                            Indira Gandhi

Asian Words of Meaning

You must learn to be still in the midst of activity and to be vibrantly alive in repose.

Indira Gandhi

Without knowing the force of words, it is impossible to know men.

Confucius

Power is of two kinds. One is obtained by the fear of punishment and the other by acts of love. Power based on love is a thousand times more effective and permanent then the one derived from fear of punishment.

Mohandas Karamchand (Mahatma) Gandhi

It is not because things are difficult that we do not dare, it is because we do not dare that they are difficult.

L. P. Sanadhya

Inspiration generates inspiration. It gives of itself to whatever it touches.

Paramahansa Yogananda

Do not wait for leaders. Do it alone, person to person.

Mother Teresa

Asian Words of Meaning

Riches are not from abundance of worldly goods, but from a contented mind.

> Prophet Muhammad

The secret of joy in work is contained in one word — excellence. To know how to do something well is to enjoy it.

> Pearl S. Buck

Tzu-kung asked about the true gentleman. Confucius said: He does not preach what he practices till he has practiced what he preaches.

> Confucius

So an ancient once said "Accept the anxieties and difficulties of this life." Don't expect your practice to be clear of obstacles. Without hindrances the mind that seeks enlightenment may be burned out. So an ancient once said "Attain deliverance in disturbances."

> Kyong Ho

He who controls others may be powerful but he who has mastered himself is mightier still.

> Lao-Tzu

Asian Words of Meaning

Remain, calm, serene, always in command of yourself. You will then find out how easy it is to get along.

                                        Paramahansa Yogananda

When you meet someone better than yourself, turn your thoughts to becoming his equal. When you meet someone not as good as you are, look within and examine your own self.

                                                          Confucius

The superior man cultivates a friendly harmony, without being weak.

                                                          Confucius

Even if you have failed at something nine times, you have still given it effort nine times.

                                                 Tibetan Proverb

The superior person is firm in the right way, and not merely firm.

                                                          Confucius

Before enlightenment chop wood and carry water. After enlightenment chop wood and carry water.

                                              Chinese Proverb

Asian Words of Meaning

Be careful what you water your dreams with. Water them with worry and fear and you will produce weeds that choke the life from your dream. Water them with optimism and solutions and you will cultivate success. Always be on the lookout for ways to turn a problem into an opportunity for success. Always be on the lookout for ways to nurture your dream.

Lao-Tzu

You cannot prevent the birds of sorrow from flying over your head, but you can prevent them from building a nest in your hair.

Chinese Proverb

Karma means action. So things change through action not by prayer, not by wish.

Dalai Lama

Conquer your foe by force, you increase his enmity; conquer by love, and you will reap no after-sorrow.

Fo-Sho-Hing-Tsan-King

In the war between falsehood and truth, falsehood often wins the first battle, but truth wins the last.

Mujibur Rahman

Asian Words of Meaning

Do you have the patience to wait till your mud settles and the water is clear? Can you remain unmoving till the right action arises by itself?

Lao-Tzu

Life is like a game of cards. The hand you are dealt with is determinism; the way you play it is free will.

Jawaharlal Nehru

Let me not pray to be sheltered from dangers, but to be fearless in facing them. Let me not beg for the stilling of my pain, but for the heart to conquer it.

Rabindranath Tagore

Each man's future is in his own hands.

Dalai Lama

Those who reach greatness on earth, reach it through concentration.

The Upanishads

Perception is strong and sight weak. In strategy, it is important to see distant things as if they were close and to take a distanced view of close things.

Miyamoto Musashi

Asian Words of Meaning

Who is not satisfied with himself will grow; who is not sure of his own correctness will learn many things.

> Chinese Proverb

Indolence is a delightful but distressing state; we must be doing something to be happy. Action is no less necessary than thought to the instinctive tendencies of the human frame.

> Mohandas Karamchand (Mahatma) Gandhi

Adaptability is not imitation. It means power of resistance and assimilation.

> Mohandas Karamchand (Mahatma) Gandhi

You can't cross the sea merely by standing and staring at the water. Don't let yourself indulge in vain wishes.

> Rabindranath Tagore

A "no" uttered from deepest conviction is better and greater than a "yes" merely uttered to please, or what is worse, to avoid trouble.

> Mohandas Karamchand (Mahatma) Gandhi

Great causes and little men go ill together.

> Jawaharlal Nehru

Asian Words of Meaning

He who sacrifices his conscience to ambition burns a picture to obtain the ashes.

Chinese Proverb

The secret of contentment is knowing how to enjoy what you have, and to be able to lose all desire for things beyond your reach.

Lin Yutang

Fear has its use but cowardice has none.

Mohandas Karamchand (Mahatma) Gandhi

Cowards can never be moral.

Mohandas Karamchand (Mahatma) Gandhi

Every little thing counts in a crisis.

Jawaharlal Nehru

Crises and deadlocks when they occur have at least this advantage, that they force us to think.

Jawaharlal Nehru

He who buys what he needs not, sells what he needs.

Japanese Proverb

Asian Words of Meaning

The person who runs away exposes himself to that very danger more than a person who sits quietly.
Jawaharlal Nehru

The expectations of life depend upon diligence; the mechanic that would perfect his work must first sharpen his tools.
Confucius

To be in good moral condition requires at least as much training as to be in good physical condition.
Jawaharlal Nehru

Loyal and efficient work in a great cause, even though it may not be immediately recognized, ultimately bears fruit.
Jawaharlal Nehru

Obviously, the highest type of efficiency is that which can utilize existing material to the best advantage.
Jawaharlal Nehru

Evil unchecked grows, evil tolerated poisons the whole system.
Jawaharlal Nehru

Asian Words of Meaning

Not the cry, but the flight of the wild duck, leads the flock to fly and follow.

Chinese Proverb

Happiness is like a sunbeam, which the least shadow intercepts, while adversity is often as the rain of spring.

Chinese Proverb

If you wish your merit to be known, acknowledge that of other people.

Chinese Proverb

Patience is power; with time and patience the mulberry leaf becomes silk.

Chinese Proverb

To see what is right, and not do it, is want of courage, or of principle.

Confucius

He who wishes to secure the good of others has already secured his own.

Confucius

Asian Words of Meaning

The effects of our actions may be postponed but they are never lost. There is an inevitable reward for good deeds and an inescapable punishment for bad. Meditate upon this truth, and seek always to earn good wages from Destiny.

Wu Ming Fu

The policy of being too cautious is the greatest risk of all.

Jawaharlal Nehru

Small ills are the fountains of most of our groans. Men trip not on mountains, they stumble on stones.

Chinese Proverb

Unity to be real must stand the severest strain without breaking.

Mohandas Karamchand (Mahatma) Gandhi

The greatest conqueror is he who overcomes the enemy without a blow.

Chinese Proverb

The person who talks most of his own virtue is often the least virtuous.

Jawaharlal Nehru

Asian Words of Meaning

Your capacity to keep your vow will depend on the purity of your life.
> Mohandas Karamchand (Mahatma) Gandhi

Personally, I hold that man who deliberately and intelligently takes a pledge and then breaks it, forfeits his manhood.
> Mohandas Karamchand (Mahatma) Gandhi

Strength does not come from physical capacity. It comes from an indomitable will.
> Mohandas Karamchand (Mahatma) Gandhi

It is unwise to be too sure of one's own wisdom. It is healthy to be reminded that the strongest might weaken and the wisest might err.
> Mohandas Karamchand (Mahatma) Gandhi

This I conceive to be the chemical function of honor; to change the character of our thought.
> Lin Yutang

The man of virtue makes the difficulty to be overcome his first business, and success only a subsequent consideration. This may be called perfect virtue.
> Confucius

Asian Words of Meaning

To show forbearance and gentleness in teaching others; and not to revenge unreasonable conduct — the good man makes it his study. To lie under arms; and meet death without regret — the forceful make it their study.

Confucius

Do not stand in a place of danger trusting in miracles.

Arabian Proverb

Each of us must make his own true way, and when we do, that way will express the universal way.

Suzuki Roshi

An insincere and evil friend is more to be feared than a wild beast. A wild beast may wound your body, but an evil friend will wound your mind.

Buddha

The spirit of democracy cannot be imposed from without. It has to come from within.

Mohandas Karamchand (Mahatma) Gandhi

People can change. Make the effort, take the time, and change yourself.

Dalai Lama

Asian Words of Meaning

Besides the noble art of getting things done, there is nobler art of leaving things undone. The wisdom of life consists in the elimination of nonessentials.

Lin Yutang

My grandfather once told me that there are two kinds of people – those who work and those who take the credit. He told me to try to be in the first group; there was less competition there.

Indira Gandhi

The only true strength is a strength that people do not fear.

Tao Te Ching

The father who does not teach his son his duties is equally guilty with the son who neglects them.

Confucius

Nothing is difficult if you are used to it.

Indonesian Proverb

Agriculture is best, enterprise is acceptable, but avoid being on a fixed wage.

Indian Proverb

Asian Words of Meaning

Fate and self-help share equally in shaping our destiny.
Indian Proverb

Keep five yards from a carriage, ten yards from a horse, and a hundred yards from an elephant; but the distance one should keep from a wicked man cannot be measured.
Indian Proverb

The way to overcome the angry man is with gentleness, the evil man with goodness, the miser with generosity, and the liar with truth.
Indian Proverb

Be not ashamed of mistakes and thus make them crimes.
Confucian Proverb

If you like things easy, you'll have difficulties; if you like problems, you'll succeed.
Laotian Proverb

Don't let anybody walk through your mind with dirty feet.
Mohandas Karamchand (Mahatma) Gandhi

Victory attained by violence is tantamount to a defeat, for it is momentary.
Mohandas Karamchand (Mahatma) Gandhi

Asian Words of Meaning

He that would have the fruit must climb the tree.
>Mohandas Karamchand (Mahatma) Gandhi

Action may not always bring happiness; but there is no happiness without action.
>Mohandas Karamchand (Mahatma) Gandhi

When anger rises, think of the consequences.
>Confucius

Dig a well before you are thirsty.
>Chinese Proverb

Determination, with an optimistic attitude, is the key factor for success.
>Dalai Lama

The way to change minds is with affection, and not anger.
>Dalai Lama

Worry not that no one knows you; seek to be worth knowing.
>Confucius

The wise man reads both books and life itself.
>Lin Yutang

Asian Words of Meaning

Among creatures some lead and some follow.
Some blow hot and some blow cold.
Some are strong and some are weak.
Some may break and some may fall.
Therefore the sage discards the extremes, the extravagant, and the excessive.

Lao-Tzu

Great is the man who has not lost his childlike heart.

Mencius

Let not a man do what his sense of right bids him not to do, nor desire what it forbids him to desire. This is sufficient. The skillful artist will not alter his measures for the sake of a stupid workman.

Mencius

Despise the enemy strategically, but take him seriously tactically.

Mao Zedong

A good traveler is one who does not know where he is going to, and a perfect traveler does not know where he came from.

Lin Yutang

Asian Words of Meaning

Hope is like a road in the country; there was never a road, but when many people walk on it, the road comes into existence.

Lin Yutang

To be idle is a short road to death and to be diligent is a way of life; foolish people are idle, wise people are diligent.

Buddha

If you look up, there are no limits.

Japanese Proverb

When prosperity comes, do not use all of it.

Confucius

Always aim at complete harmony of thought and word and deed. Always aim at purifying your thoughts and everything will be well.

Mohandas Karamchand (Mahatma) Gandhi

You don't have to be a fantastic hero to do certain things; to compete. You can be just an ordinary person, sufficiently motivated to reach challenging goals. The intense effort, the giving of everything you've got, is a very pleasant side effect.

Sir Edmond Hillary

Asian Words of Meaning

Before changing others, we ourselves must change. We must be honest, sincere, kind-hearted.

Dalai Lama

In fighting and in everyday life you should be determined though calm. Do not let the enemy see your spirit.

Miyamoto Musashi

Although gold dust is precious, when it gets in your eyes, it obstructs your vision.

Hsi-Tang

Wheresoever you go, go with all your heart.

Confucius

Be the first to the field and the last to the couch.

Chinese Proverb

What we are today comes from our thoughts of yesterday, and our present thoughts build our life of tomorrow. Our life is a creation of our mind.

Buddha

Work out your own salvation. Do not depend on others.

Buddha

Asian Words of Meaning

Ambition never comes to an end.
Yoshida Kenkō

So much restlessness is due to the fact that a man does not know what he wants, or he wants too many things, or perhaps he wants to be somebody else, to be anybody except himself.
Lin Yutang

Always keep your mind as bright and clear as the vast sky, the great ocean, and the highest peak, empty of all thoughts. Always keep your body filled with light and heat. Fill yourself with the power of wisdom and enlightenment.
Morihei Ueshiba

Infinite striving to be the best is man's duty, and its own reward.
Mohandas Karamchand (Mahatma) Gandhi

There are three sorts of friends that are profitable, and three sorts that are harmful. Friendship with the upright, with the true-to-death, and with those who have heard much is profitable. Friendship with the obsequious, with those who are good at accommodating their principles, or those who are clever at talk is harmful.
Confucius

Asian Words of Meaning

Possession of material riches without inner peace is like dying of thirst while bathing in a lake.

        Paramahansa Yogananda

There is nothing more yielding than water, yet when acting on the solid and strong, its gentleness and fluidity have no equal in anything. The weak can overcome the strong, and the supple overcome the hard. Although this is known far and wide, few put it into practice in their lives.

        Lao-Tzu

Work performed with attachment is a shackle, whereas work performed with detachment does not affect the doer. He is, even while working, in solitude.

        Sri Ramana Maharshi

The person of integrity wafts a scent in every direction.

        Dhammapada

Whatever you find hardest to do, do with all your heart.

        Dalai Lama

Never was good work done without much trouble.

        Chinese Proverb

Asian Words of Meaning

Don't be disquieted in time of adversity. Be firm with dignity and self-reliant with vigor.

Chiang Kai-shek

The perfecting of one's self is the fundamental base of all progress and all moral development.

Confucius

Desire excites. Excitement may sometimes elevate us but will depress us eventually. Inspiration elevates further and further.

Swami Amar Jyoti

Ask yourself constantly, "What is the right thing to do?"

Confucius

The person who removes a mountain begins by carrying away small stones.

Chinese Proverb

He who will not economize will have to agonize.

Confucius

The superior man has neither anxiety nor fear.

Confucius

Asian Words of Meaning

The whole secret of existence is to have no fear. Never fear what will become of you, depend on no one. Only the moment you reject all help are you freed.
Buddha

Our greatest glory is not in never falling, but in rising every time we fall.
Confucius

I don't wait for moods. You accomplish nothing if you do that. Your mind must know it has got to get down to work.
Pearl S. Buck

The great virtue of man lies in his ability to correct his mistakes and continually to make a new man of himself.
Wang Yang-Ming

As the water shapes itself to the vessel that contains it, so a wise man adapts himself to circumstances.
Confucius

Seek not happiness too greedily, and be not fearful of unhappiness.
Lao-Tzu

Asian Words of Meaning

The determination to win is the better part of winning.

Daisaku Ikeda

Only those who can be strict with themselves hold the key to coming out on top.

Umeo Oyama

Life's fulfillment finds constant contradictions in its path; but those are necessary for the sake of its advance. The stream is saved from the sluggishness of its current by the perpetual opposition of the soil through which it must cut its way. It is the soil which forms its banks. The Spirit of fight belongs to the genius of life.

Rabindranath Tagore

The thought manifests as the word. The word manifests as the deed. The deed develops into habit. And the habit hardens into character. So watch the thought and its ways with care. And let it spring from love, born out of concern for all beings.

Buddha

Whatever is flexible and loving will tend to grow; whatever is rigid and blocked will wither and die.

Lao-Tzu

Asian Words of Meaning

To fight and conquer in all your battles is not supreme excellence. Supreme excellence consists of prevailing over the enemy without fighting.

Sun Tzu

Roll logs down a ten-thousand foot mountain, and they cannot be stopped. This is because of the mountain, not the logs. So it is with the force generated by superior strategy and position. Victorious generals seek victory in battle from strategy and position, not from the abilities of their officers or soldiers.

Sun Tzu

Be vigilant; guard your mind against negative thoughts.

Buddha

Sometimes it is more important to discover what one cannot do than what one can do.

Lin Yutang

Virtue is not left to stand alone. He who practices it will have neighbors.

Confucius

Asian Words of Meaning

Discard little wisdom and great wisdom will become clear.

                                                                            Chuang Tzu

It does not matter how slowly you go, as long as you do not stop.

                                                                            Confucius

Like a beautiful flower that is colorful but has no fragrance, even well spoken words bear no fruit in one who does not put them into practice.

                                                                            Buddha

An ant on the move does more than a dozing ox.

                                                                            Lao-Tzu

Asian Words of Meaning

Caring & Service to Others

Service to others, especially to one's neighbors and community, is embedded in many Asian cultures. This has easily migrated into the business world throughout the region, as can be witnessed in the hospitality, aviation, and tourism industries all across Asia.

Though not of Asian descent, Mother Teresa is probably the person who best exemplifies the concept of service to others in recent Asian history. This is why we have included several quotes and phrases from this Macedonia-born nun, for she will forever be linked with Asia and her humanitarian work in India.

Another good example is Singaporean Kwok Wai Min, who devoted his spare time to building houses in Sri Lanka for the victims of the Indian Ocean tsunami that devastated this region in December 2004. There were thousands of stories of Asians helping other Asians, serving both their fellow countrymen and their regional neighbors, emanating from the shocking and destructive tidal waves that shattered and destroyed so many communities on that fateful day.

Asian Words of Meaning

It is this kind of service — to one's fellow man and neighbor — that the Asian sages have spoken so eloquently about through the years. As the quotations below show, altruism is at the very foundation of every Asian society.

In my own personal philosophy, service to others is one of the ten building blocks to a balanced and fulfilling life. While I could never emulate Mother Teresa, or even Kwok Wai Min for that matter, I do try to give back to my community, and the world at large, through contributions of my time, experiences, skills, and money.

I hope the words below will encourage and motivate you to add caring and service to others as one of your own foundation blocks in building your own fulfilling life.

Do not think that love, in order to be genuine, has to be extraordinary. What we need is to love without getting tired.
Mother Teresa

The fragrance always remains on the hand that gives the rose.
Mohandas Karamchand (Mahatma) Gandhi

Asian Words of Meaning

Kindness in giving creates love.

> Lao-Tzu

Consideration for others is the basis of a good life, a good society.

> Confucius

One can pay back the loan of gold, but one dies forever in debt to those who are kind.

> Malay Proverb

God doesn't look at how much we do, but with how much love we do it.

> Mother Teresa

There is a magnet in your heart that will attract true friends. That magnet is unselfishness, thinking of others first. When you learn to live for others, they will live for you.

> Paramahansa Yogananda

Teach this triple truth to all: A generous heart, kind speech, and a life of service and compassion are the things which renew humanity.

> Buddha

Asian Words of Meaning

If you can't feed a hundred people, then feed just one.

Mother Teresa

There should be less talk. What do you do then? Take a broom and clean someone's house. That says enough.

Mother Teresa

Be kind whenever possible. It is always possible.

Dalai Lama

We live very close together. So, our prime purpose in this life is to help others. And if you can't help them, at least don't hurt them.

Dalai Lama

Think of the poorest person you have ever seen and ask if your next act will be of any use to him.

Mohandas Karamchand (Mahatma) Gandhi

Everyone has a purpose in life….a unique gift or special talent to give to others. And when we blend this unique talent with service to others, we experience the ecstasy and exultation of our own spirit, which is the ultimate goal of all goals.

Deepak Chopra

Asian Words of Meaning

May I become at all times, both now and forever,
a protector for those without protection
a guide for those who have lost their way
a ship for those with oceans to cross
a bridge for those with rivers to cross
a sanctuary for those in danger
a lamp for those who need light
a place of refuge for those needing shelter
and a servant to all those in need.

Dalai Lama

Condemn none: if you can stretch out a helping hand, do so. If you cannot, fold your hands, bless your brothers, and let them go their own way.

Swami Vivekananda

Surrender yourself humbly; then you can be trusted to care for all things. Love the world as your own self; then you can truly care for all things.

Lao-Tzu

There is no need for temples, no need for complicated philosophies. My brain and my heart are my temples; my philosophy is kindness.

Dalai Lama

Asian Words of Meaning

The greatest help or service you can do to the world is the imparting of knowledge of the Self. Spiritual help is the highest help you can render to mankind. The root cause of human sufferings is ignorance. If you can remove this ignorance in man, then only can he be eternally happy. That sage who tries to remove the ignorance is the highest benefactor in the world.

Swami Sivananda Saraswati

Patience shown to the unworthy is the means of polishing the worthy: wherever a heart exists, patience purifies it.

Rumi

My life is an indivisible whole, and all my attitudes run into one another; and they all have their rise in my insatiable love for mankind.

Mohandas Karamchand (Mahatma) Gandhi

Some help others in order to receive blessings and admiration. This is simply meaningless. Some cultivate themselves in part to serve others, in part to serve their own pride. They will understand, at best, half of the truth. But those who improve themselves for the sake of the world — to these, the whole truth of the universe will be revealed.

Lao-Tzu

Asian Words of Meaning

A positive state of mind is not merely good for you, it benefits everyone with whom you come into contact, literally changing the world.

Dalai Lama

If you light a lamp for someone else it will also brighten your path.

Buddha

A vow is fixed and unalterable determination to do a thing, when such a determination is related to something noble which can only uplift the man who makes the resolve.

Mohandas Karamchand (Mahatma) Gandhi

I alone cannot change the world, but I can cast a stone across the waters to create many ripples.

Mother Teresa

Giving connects two people, the giver and the receiver, and this connection gives birth to a new sense of belonging.

Deepak Chopra

If you knew what I know about the power of giving, you would not let a single meal pass without sharing it in some way.

Buddha

Asian Words of Meaning

When you have understood that all existence, in separation and limitation, is painful, and when you are willing and able to live integrally, in oneness with all life, as pure being, you have gone beyond all need of help. You can help another by precept and example and, above all, by your being. You cannot give what you do not have and you don't have what you are not. You can only give what you are — and of that you can give limitlessly.

Nisargadatta Maharaj

When you plant lettuce, if it does not grow well, you don't blame the lettuce. You look for reasons it is not doing well. It may need fertilizer, or more water, or less sun. You never blame the lettuce. Yet if we have problems with our friends or family, we blame the other person. But if we know how to take care of them, they will grow well, like the lettuce. Blaming has no positive effect at all, nor does trying to persuade using reason and argument. That is my experience. No blame, no reasoning, no argument, just understanding. If you understand, and you show that you understand, you can love, and the situation will change.

Thich Nhat Hanh

Asian Words of Meaning

Accept disgrace willingly. Accept misfortune as the human condition. What do I mean by "Accept disgrace willingly?" Accept being unimportant. Do not be concerned with loss or gain. This is called "accepting disgrace willingly." What do I mean by "Accept misfortune as the human condition?" Misfortune comes from having a body. Without a body, how could there be misfortune? Surrender yourself humbly; then you can be trusted to care for all things. Love the world as your own self; then you can truly care for all things.

Lao-Tzu

Thousands of candles can be lighted from a single candle, and the life of the candle will not be shortened. Happiness never decreases by being shared.

Chinese Proverb

Anything that is of value in life only multiplies when it is given.

Deepak Chopra

When you desire the common good, the whole world desires with you. Make humanity's desire your own and work for it. There you cannot fail.

Nisargadatta Maharaj

Asian Words of Meaning

To give pleasure to a single heart by a single act is better than a thousand heads bowing in prayer.
> Mohandas Karamchand (Mahatma) Gandhi

When you are laboring for others let it be with the same zeal as if it were for yourself.
> Confucius

Let the motive be in the deed and not in the event. Be not one whose motive for action is the hope of reward.
> Krishna

Birdsong brings relief to my longing. I am just as ecstatic as they are, but with nothing to say! Please, universal soul, practice some song, or something, through me!
> Rumi

One generation plants the trees; another gets the shade.
> Chinese Proverb

Anger ends in cruelty.
> Indian Proverb

Friendship is one mind in two bodies.
> Mencius

Asian Words of Meaning

Never overlook wallflower at dance; may be dandelion in grass.

               Confucius

Kindly words do not enter so deeply into men as a reputation for kindness.

               Mencius

Today we are afraid of simple words like goodness and mercy and kindness. We don't believe in the good old words because we don't believe in good old values anymore. And that's why the world is sick.

               Lin Yutang

The hunger for love is much more difficult to remove than the hunger for bread.

               Mother Teresa

I have found the paradox, that if you love until it hurts, there can be no more hurt, only more love.

               Mother Teresa

Being deeply loved by someone gives you strength; loving someone deeply gives you courage.

               Lao-Tzu

Asian Words of Meaning

When the sense of distinction and separation is absent, you may call it love.

                                          Nisargadatta Maharaj

The more we come out and do good to others, the more our hearts will be purified, and God will be in them.

                                          Swami Vivekananda

Every day, think as you wake up, today I am fortunate to be alive, I have a precious human life, I am not going to waste it. I am going to use all my energies to develop myself, to expand my heart out to others; to achieve enlightenment for the benefit of all beings. I am going to have kind thoughts towards others, I am not going to get angry or think badly about others. I am going to benefit others as much as I can.

                                          Dalai Lama

I am a little pencil in the hand of a writing God who is sending a love letter to the world.

                                          Mother Teresa

Kind words can be short and easy to speak, but their echoes are truly endless.

                                          Mother Teresa

Asian Words of Meaning

I believe all suffering is caused by ignorance. People inflict pain on others in the selfish pursuit of their happiness or satisfaction. Yet true happiness comes from a sense of peace and contentment, which in turn must be achieved through the cultivation of altruism, of love and compassion, and elimination of ignorance, selfishness, and greed.
Dalai Lama

A man's true wealth is the good he does in the world.
Prophet Muhammad

Why are you unhappy? Because 99.9% of what you think, and everything you do, is for yourself. And there isn't one.
Wu Wei Wu

The best relationship is one in which your love for each other exceeds your need for each other.
Dalai Lama

One who knows the truth sees everyone else as a manifestation of God.
Sri Ramana Maharshi

The way to others' minds is with affection, not anger.
Dalai Lama

Asian Words of Meaning

If you see good in people, you radiate a harmonious loving energy which uplifts those who are around you. If you can maintain this habit, this energy will turn into a steady flow of love.

Annamalai Swami

Kindness in words creates confidence. Kindness in thinking creates profoundness. Kindness in giving creates love.

Lao-Tzu

Behave toward everyone as if receiving a great guest.

Confucius

Let my soul smile through my heart and my heart smile through my eyes, that I may scatter rich smiles in sad hearts.

Paramahansa Yogananda

The best way to find yourself is to lose yourself in the service of others.

Mohandas Karamchand (Mahatma) Gandhi

Go out into the world today and love the people you meet. Let your presence light new light in the hearts of people.

Mother Teresa

Asian Words of Meaning

Fashion your life as a garland of beautiful deeds.
>Buddha

To receive anything, one must open one's hands and give.
>Taisen Deshimaru

The greatest lessons in life, if we would but stoop and humble ourselves, we should learn not from the grown-up learned men, but from the so-called ignorant children.
>Mohandas Karamchand (Mahatma) Gandhi

Happiness comes when your work and words are of benefit to yourself and others.
>Buddha

Your pride in yourself and your wanting, these steal your energy along the road. If you can kill these robbers and become the servant of everyone, you'll meet the source and see what you used to protect as just a pile of ashes.
>Lalla

In the perception of the smallest is the secret of clear vision; in the guarding of the weakest is the secret of all strength.
>Lao-Tzu

Asian Words of Meaning

Let no one come to you without going away better and happier. Be the living expression of God's kindness: kindness in your face, kindness in your eyes, kindness in your smile, kindness in your warm greeting. Give them not only your care, but also your heart.

Mother Teresa

If you want happiness for an hour, take a nap.
If you want happiness for a day, go fishing.
If you want happiness for a year, inherit a fortune.
If you want happiness for a lifetime, help somebody.

Chinese Proverb

Help thy brother's boat across, and lo! — thine own has reached the shore.

Hindu Proverb

Even an unadaptable man who is completely useless is a most trusted retainer if all he does is nothing more than think earnestly of his lord's welfare.

Miyamoto Musashi

Perfect kindness acts without thinking of kindness.

Lao-Tzu

Asian Words of Meaning

Ideally, one should have a great deal of courage and strength, but not boast or make a big show of it. Then, in times of need, one should rise to the occasion and fight bravely for what is right.

Dalai Lama

If we have no peace, it is because we have forgotten that we belong to each other.

Mother Teresa

Where there is love there is life.

Mohandas Karamchand (Mahatma) Gandhi

It suits the generous person to give money but the true generosity of the lover is to surrender their soul.

Rumi

When we feel love and kindness towards others, it not only makes others feel loved and cared for, but it helps us also to develop inner happiness and peace.

Dalai Lama

Kindness is the light that dissolves all walls between souls, families, and nations.

Paramahansa Yogananda

Asian Words of Meaning

The roots of all goodness lie in the soil of appreciation for goodness.

Dalai Lama

About the Author

Steven Howard
Global Leadership Development and Facilitation
Leadership Coach | Keynote Speaker

Steven Howard specializes in creating and delivering Leadership Development curriculum for frontline leaders, mid-level leaders, senior leaders and high-potential leaders.

An author with 36 years of international senior sales, marketing, and leadership experience, his corporate career covered a wide variety of fields and experiences, including Regional Marketing Director for Texas Instruments Asia-Pacific, South Asia & ASEAN Regional Director for TIME Magazine, Global Account Director at BBDO Advertising handling an international airline account, and VP Marketing for Citibank's Consumer Banking Group.

Since 1988 he has delivered leadership development training programs in the U.S., Asia, Australia, Africa, Canada, and Europe to numerous organizations, including Citicorp, Covidien, DBS Bank, Deutsche Bank, DuPont Lycra, Esso Productions, ExxonMobil, Hewlett Packard Enterprise,

Asian Words of Meaning

Micron Technology, Motorola Inc., Motorola Solutions, SapientNitro, Standard Chartered Bank, and many others.

He has been a member of the training faculty at MasterCard University Asia/Pacific, the Citibank Asia-Pacific Banking Institute, and Forum Corporation. He brings a truly international, cross-cultural perspective to his leadership development programs, having lived in the USA for 26 years, in Singapore for 21 years and in Australia for 12 years.

In addition to his leadership facilitation work Steven has served on several Boards in both the private and non-profit sectors. He has also chaired a strategic advisory group for a local government entity and a national sporting organization that is a member of the Australian Olympic Committee.

Steven is the author of 16 marketing, management, and leadership books and is the editor of three professional and personal development books in the *Project You* series.

His books are:

> ***Corporate Image Management:*** *A Marketing Discipline*
>
> ***Powerful Marketing Minutes:*** *50 Ways to Develop Market Leadership*
>
> ***MORE Powerful Marketing Minutes:*** *50 New Ways to Develop Market Leadership*

Asian Words of Meaning

Asian Words of Wisdom

Asian Words of Knowledge

Essential Asian Words of Wisdom

Pillars of Growth: *Strategies for Leading Sustainable Growth* (co-author with three others)

Motivation Plus Marketing Equals Money (co-author with four others)

Marketing Words of Wisdom

The Best of the Monday Morning Marketing Memo

Powerful Marketing Memos

8 Keys To Becoming A Great Leader *(With Leadership Lessons and Tips from Gibbs, Yoda and Capt'n Jack Sparrow)*

Asian Words of Success

Asian Words of Meaning

Asian Words of Inspiration

The Book of Asian Proverbs

Asian Words of Meaning

Contact Details
Email: steven@CalienteLeadership.com

Twitter: @stevenbhoward | @GreatLeadershp

LinkedIn: www.linkedin.com/in/stevenbhoward

Facebook: www.facebook.com/CalienteLeadership

Website: www.CalienteLeadership.com

Blog: CalienteLeadership.com/TheArtofGreatLeadershipBlog

Asian Words of Meaning

Reader Reviews Appreciated

Thank you for reading this book. I hope you found some useful nuggets of wisdom that are relevant to your current and future life journey.

One favor to ask, if I may. Please take a few minutes, go to this book's page on Amazon and leave a reader review. Here's the link: http://www.amazon.com/dp/B01LM0JZJ8.

As an author I sincerely appreciate hearing from my readers. And I know other readers often use these reviews in determining whether a book might meet their needs.

Thank you in advance.

And best wishes for continued success in your professional and personal endeavors.

Asian Words of Meaning

www.ingramcontent.com/pod-product-compliance
Lightning Source LLC
Chambersburg PA
CBHW071315060426
42444CB00036B/2776